THE BAKING
Collection

THE AUSTRALIAN
Women's Weekly

THE BAKING
Collection

BAUER

CONTENTS

THE BAKING
Collection

Baking is what we love most in the Australian Women's Weekly Test Kitchen. It is what we're famous for. This new collection is full of our well-known, much-loved – and fail-safe – baking recipes, with plenty of helpful tips and hints to guide you to baking excellence. Biscuits and slices are perfect for lunchboxes, gifts and just about any occasion you can think of. Slices are a particular favourite – they're often faster to make than biscuits and can be cut to a size to suit their purpose. To keep slices fresh for longer, cut into pieces as you need them – this reduces the cut surface area, which in turn reduces staling and drying out.

Teacakes and pikelets are best made at the last minute and served warm. Teacakes and their cousins – coffeecakes – rarely contain tea or coffee, they're meant to be served with either beverage. Pikelets are a perfect standby – they're easy to make and you can whip them up while you're chatting to those pop-in guests. Serve them with butter and jam, or jam and whipped cream. They don't keep well, but they will freeze quite happily and thaw in no time.

Everybody loves cakes and sponges – they're the perfect blend of art and science. To consistently make good cakes, keep on practising – weigh, measure and follow the recipes carefully, and turn cakes halfway through baking time for even browning – it's all about experience when it comes to cakes.

Pastries and whoopie pies, particularly pastries, take a bit of time to make, but they are worth the effort. Whoopie pies are a cross between a cake, a muffin and a rock cake – they come in pairs and are joined with a filling of some sort. Don't worry if they're not perfect in size and shape – the rustic look is part of their charm.

Puddings and pies – in other words, sweets or desserts – depending on where you come from. There are classic and modern recipes here, we've used many different types of pastry, some commercially-made others home-made.

The bread recipes in this book have leapt many culinary fences, from Aussie damper through to Middle-Eastern pide. If you haven't handled yeast before, promise yourself to make your own bread or hot cross buns just once for the experience – you'll be hooked.

Tiny and tempting, is where you'll find an amazing array of sweet treats including truffles, petit fours, confectionery, madeleines, cupcakes, friands, muffins and so on.

Special occasions are the perfect opportunity for you to test your skills. From little Christmas cupcakes, to the most breath-taking birthday cake, these recipes have that extra bit of sparkle.

Everyone from novice to master will find something delicious here to bake. And, remember once you understand the basics about baking, anything and everything is possible.

CHAPTER 1
BISCUITS
& SLICES

RASPBERRY AND CINNAMON
French Macaroons

PREP + COOK TIME *1 HOUR 15 MINUTES (+ REFRIGERATION, STANDING & COOLING)* MAKES *20*

3 egg whites
¼ cup (55g) caster (superfine) sugar
1¼ cups (200g) icing (confectioners') sugar
1 cup (120g) ground almonds
½ teaspoon ground cinnamon

RASPBERRY ROSE BUTTERCREAM
150g (4½ ounces) unsalted butter, chopped coarsely
½ cup (80g) icing (confectioners') sugar
⅓ cup (110g) raspberry conserve
½ teaspoon rosewater

CINNAMON SUGAR
2 tablespoons icing (confectioners') sugar
½ teaspoon ground cinnamon

1　Make raspberry rose buttercream.
2　Make cinnamon sugar.
3　Grease oven trays; line with baking paper.
4　Beat egg whites in a small bowl with an electric mixer until soft peaks form. Add caster sugar; beat until sugar is dissolved. Transfer mixture to a large bowl. Fold in sifted icing sugar, ground almonds and cinnamon, in two batches.
5　Spoon the mixture into a piping bag fitted with a 2cm (¾-inch) plain tube. Pipe 4cm (1½-inch) rounds about 2cm (¾ inch) apart on trays. Tap trays on bench so macaroons spread slightly. Dust macaroons with half the sifted cinnamon sugar; stand about 30 minutes or until dry to touch.
6　Meanwhile, preheat oven to 150°C/300°F.
7　Bake macaroons about 20 minutes; cool on trays.
8　Sandwich macaroons with buttercream; dust with remaining sifted cinnamon sugar.

RASPBERRY ROSE BUTTERCREAM
Beat butter and icing sugar in a small bowl with an electric mixer about 3 minutes or until pale and fluffy. Push raspberry conserve through a fine sieve; discard seeds. Add sieved conserve and rosewater to butter mixture; beat until combined.

CINNAMON SUGAR
Combine ingredients in a small bowl.

Unfilled macaroons will keep in an airtight container for about a week. Filled macaroons will keep in an airtight container in the fridge for up to two days.

STRAWBERRY AND CREAM
Cookies

PREP + COOK TIME *1 HOUR 30 MINUTES (+ FREEZING)* **MAKES** *40*

1 vanilla bean
250g (8 ounces) butter, softened
1 cup (220g) caster (superfine) sugar
1 egg
2½ cups (375g) plain (all-purpose) flour
2 teaspoons strawberry essence
pink food colouring
125g (4 ounces) white eating chocolate,
    chopped coarsely

1 Split the vanilla bean in half lengthways; scrape
   out the seeds. Discard pod or save for another
   use (see notes).
2 Beat butter, sugar and vanilla seeds in a medium
   bowl with an electric mixer until light and fluffy.
   Beat in egg. Stir in 2⅓ cups of the sifted flour.
   Knead dough on floured surface until smooth.
3 Divide dough in half. Return half the dough to the
   bowl; stir in essence and remaining sifted flour.
   Tint pink with colouring.
4 Divide the vanilla and strawberry doughs in half.
   On a floured surface, shape each portion of dough
   into 30cm (12-inch) logs (you will have two vanilla
   and two strawberry logs). Twist one vanilla and
   one strawberry log together to create a marbled
   effect; smooth into a neat log again. Repeat with
   remaining logs (you will have two marbled logs).
   Wrap logs in baking paper; freeze about 2 hours or
   until firm.

5 Remove logs from freezer; set aside for 15 minutes
   to soften slightly.
6 Meanwhile, preheat oven to 180°C/350°F. Line oven
   trays with baking paper.
7 Cut logs into 1cm (½-inch) slices; place about 3cm
   (1¼ inches) apart on trays.
8 Bake biscuits about 13 minutes. Stand 5 minutes
   on tray before transferring biscuits to a wire rack
   over another oven tray. Cool.
9 Stir chocolate in a small heatproof bowl over a
   small saucepan of simmering water until melted.
   Spoon chocolate into a plastic resealable bag;
   snip off one corner and pipe chocolate into spiral
   or zigzag patterns on biscuits. Stand at room
   temperature until chocolate is set.

Place the unused vanilla pod in a jar of caster sugar
to make your own vanilla sugar.
These biscuits will keep in an airtight container for
up to a week.

CHOCOLATE AND FIG
Biscotti

PREP + COOK TIME *1 HOUR (+ REFRIGERATION)* MAKES *ABOUT 30*

1 cup (190g) coarsely chopped dried figs
¼ cup (60ml) orange-flavoured liqueur
30g (1 ounce) butter, softened
½ cup (110g) firmly packed light brown sugar
1 teaspoon vanilla extract
3 eggs
1¼ cups (185g) plain (all-purpose) flour
⅓ cup (35g) cocoa powder
½ teaspoon baking powder
150g (4½ ounces) dark eating (semi-sweet)
  chocolate, chopped finely

1 Combine figs and liqueur in a medium bowl. Cover; stand 1 hour.

2 Beat butter, sugar and extract in a small bowl with an electric mixer until combined. Beat in eggs, one at a time (mixture may separate at this stage, but will come together later). Stir in sifted dry ingredients, then fig mixture and chocolate. Cover; refrigerate 1 hour.

3 Preheat oven to 180°C/350°F. Grease oven trays.

4 Divide the dough in half. Shape each portion into a 20cm (8-inch) log; place on trays.

5 Bake about 25 minutes. Cool on trays.

6 Reduce oven to 160°C/325°F.

7 Using serrated knife, cut logs diagonally into 1cm (½-inch) slices. Place slices on baking-paper-lined oven trays; bake about 30 minutes, turning halfway through cooking. Cool on wire racks.

These biscotti will keep in an airtight container for up to a week.

HAZELNUT MOMENTS
with Choc-berry Filling

PREP + COOK TIME *30 MINUTES (+ REFRIGERATION & COOLING)* **MAKES 24**

90g (3 ounces) butter, softened
½ teaspoon vanilla extract
¼ cup (55g) caster (superfine) sugar
1 egg
½ cup (50g) ground hazelnuts
¾ cup (110g) plain (all-purpose) flour
¼ cup (25g) cocoa powder

CHOC-BERRY FILLING

90g (3 ounces) dark eating (semi-sweet)
   chocolate, chopped coarsely
60g (2 ounces) butter, softened
⅓ cup (110g) chocolate-hazelnut spread
¼ cup (35g) fresh raspberries, chopped

1 Beat butter, extract, sugar and egg in a small bowl with an electric mixer until combined. Stir in ground hazelnuts, then sifted flour and cocoa.
2 Divide dough in half; roll each half between sheets of baking paper until 3mm (⅛-inch) thick. Place on tray; refrigerate 30 minutes.
3 Preheat oven to 180°C/350°F. Line oven trays with baking paper.
4 Cut 4cm (1½-inch) fluted rounds from dough; place on trays about 2.5cm (1 inch) apart.
5 Bake biscuits about 8 minutes. Cool on trays.
6 Make choc-berry filling.
7 Spoon choc-berry filling into a piping bag fitted with 2cm (¾-inch) fluted tube. Pipe filling onto flat side of half the biscuits; top with remaining biscuits.

CHOC-BERRY FILLING

Stir chocolate in a small heatproof bowl over a small saucepan of simmering water until melted. Cool. Beat cooled chocolate, butter and spread in a small bowl with an electric mixer until thick and glossy. Fold in raspberries.

Unfilled biscuits will keep in an airtight container for up to a week. Filled biscuits will keep for a few days in an airtight container in the fridge.

MONTE CARLOS

PREP + COOK TIME *1 HOUR* MAKES *25*

185g (6 ounces) butter, softened
1 teaspoon vanilla extract
½ cup (110g) firmly packed light brown sugar
1 egg
1¼ cups (185g) self-raising flour
¾ cup (110g) plain (all-purpose) flour
½ cup (40g) desiccated coconut
¼ cup (80g) raspberry jam

CREAM FILLING
60g (2 ounces) butter
½ teaspoon vanilla extract
¾ cup (120g) icing (confectioners') sugar
2 teaspoons milk

1 Preheat oven to 180°C/350°F. Grease oven trays.
2 Beat butter, extract, sugar and egg in a small bowl with an electric mixer until smooth. Transfer mixture to a large bowl; stir in sifted flours and coconut, in two batches.
3 Roll rounded teaspoons of mixture into oval shapes; place about 2.5cm (1 inch) apart on trays. Flatten slightly; rough surface with fork.
4 Bake biscuits about 12 minutes. Cool on wire racks.
5 Make cream filling.
6 Sandwich biscuits with jam and filling.

CREAM FILLING
Beat butter, extract and sifted icing sugar in a small bowl with an electric mixer until light and fluffy; beat in milk.

Unfilled biscuits will keep in an airtight container for up to a week. Filled biscuits will keep for a few days in an airtight container in the fridge.

CHOCOLATE CHIP
Cookies

PREP + COOK TIME *30 MINUTES* MAKES *36*

250g (8 ounces) butter, softened
1 teaspoon vanilla extract
¾ cup (165g) caster (superfine) sugar
¾ cup (165g) firmly packed light brown sugar
1 egg
2¼ cups (335g) plain (all-purpose) flour
1 teaspoon bicarbonate of soda (baking soda)
375g (12 ounces) dark chocolate Melts,
    chopped coarsely

1 Preheat oven to 180°C/350°F. Grease oven trays.
2 Beat butter, extract, sugars and egg in a small bowl with an electric mixer until light and fluffy. Transfer mixture to a large bowl; stir in sifted flour and soda, in two batches. Stir in chocolate.
3 Roll tablespoons of mixture into balls; place about 5cm (2 inches) apart on trays.
4 Bake biscuits about 15 minutes; cool on trays.

Dark chocolate can be replaced with milk or white chocolate.
For choc-nut cookies, replace one third of the chocolate with roasted chopped nuts such as hazelnuts, walnuts, pecans or macadamias.
These cookies will keep in an airtight container for up to a week.

MONTE CARLOS

CHOCOLATE CHIP
Cookies

PEANUT BUTTER
Cookies

PEANUT BUTTER
Cookies

PREP + COOK TIME *25 MINUTES* **MAKES** *30*

125g (4 ounces) butter, softened
¼ cup (70g) crunchy peanut butter
¾ cup (165g) firmly packed light brown sugar
1 egg
1½ cups (225g) plain (all-purpose) flour
½ teaspoon bicarbonate of soda (baking soda)
½ cup (70g) roasted unsalted peanuts,
   chopped coarsely

1 Preheat oven to 180°C/350°F. Grease oven trays;
   line with baking paper.
2 Beat butter, peanut butter, sugar and egg in a small
   bowl with an electric mixer until smooth (do not
   over-mix). Transfer mixture to a medium bowl;
   stir in sifted flour and soda, then nuts.
3 Roll level tablespoons of mixture into balls;
   place about 5cm (2 inches) apart on trays,
   flatten with a floured fork.
4 Bake cookies about 12 minutes; cool on trays.

These biscuits will keep in an airtight container
for up to a week.

GINGERNUTS

PREP + COOK TIME *30 MINUTES (+ COOLING)* **MAKES** *32*

90g (3 ounces) butter
⅓ cup (75g) firmly packed light brown sugar
⅓ cup (115g) golden syrup or treacle
1⅓ cups (200g) plain (all-purpose) flour
¾ teaspoon bicarbonate of soda (baking soda)
1 tablespoon ground ginger
1 teaspoon ground cinnamon
¼ teaspoon ground cloves

1 Preheat oven to 180°C/350°F. Grease oven trays;
   line with baking paper.
2 Stir butter, sugar and syrup in a medium saucepan
   over low heat until smooth. Remove from heat;
   stir in sifted dry ingredients. Cool 10 minutes.
3 Roll rounded teaspoons of mixture into balls.
   Place about 3cm (1¼ inches) apart on trays;
   flatten slightly.
4 Bake biscuits about 10 minutes; cool on trays.

These biscuits will keep in an airtight container
for up to a week.

(PHOTOGRAPH PAGE 22)

GINGERNUTS

(RECIPE PAGE 21)

ANZAC BISCUITS

(RECIPE PAGE 24)

ANZAC BISCUITS

PREP + COOK TIME *30 MINUTES* **MAKES** *25*

1 cup (90g) rolled oats
1 cup (150g) plain (all-purpose) flour
1 cup (220g) firmly packed light brown sugar
½ cup (40g) desiccated coconut
125g (4 ounces) butter
2 tablespoons golden syrup or treacle
1 tablespoon water
½ teaspoon bicarbonate of soda (baking soda)

1 Preheat oven to 160°C/325°F. Grease oven trays; line with baking paper.
2 Combine oats, sifted flour, sugar and coconut in a large bowl.
3 Stir butter, syrup and the water in a small saucepan over low heat until smooth; stir in soda. Stir mixture into dry ingredients.
4 Roll level tablespoons of mixture into balls; place about 5cm (2 inches) apart on trays, flatten slightly.
5 Bake biscuits about 20 minutes; cool on trays.

These biscuits will keep in an airtight container for up to a week.

(PHOTOGRAPH PAGE 23)

MACAROON
Jam Drops

PREP + COOK TIME *1 HOUR 15 MINUTES* **MAKES** *26*

2 egg whites
½ cup (110g) caster (superfine) sugar
1¼ cups (125g) ground almonds
2 tablespoons plain (all-purpose) flour
2 tablespoons raspberry jam

1 Preheat oven to 120°C/250°F. Grease oven trays; line with baking paper.
2 Beat egg whites in a small bowl with an electric mixer until soft peaks form. Gradually add sugar, beating until sugar dissolves. Fold in ground almonds and sifted flour, in two batches.
3 Drop level tablespoons of mixture, about 5cm (2 inches) apart, onto trays. Using wet finger, make a shallow hole in the centre of each macaroon. Spoon ¼ teaspoon of jam into each hole.
4 Bake macaroons about 1 hour; cool on trays.

You can use any flavoured jam you have on hand. These macaroons will keep in an airtight container for up to three days.

MACAROON
Jam Drops

GINGERBREAD PEOPLE

PREP + COOK TIME *50 MINUTES* MAKES *20*

125g (4 ounces) butter
⅓ cup (75g) firmly packed light brown sugar
½ cup (175g) golden syrup or treacle
3 cups (450g) plain (all-purpose) flour
2 teaspoons ground ginger
2 teaspoons ground cinnamon
½ teaspoon ground cloves
2 teaspoons bicarbonate of soda (baking soda)
1 egg, beaten lightly
1 teaspoon vanilla extract

ROYAL ICING

1 egg white
1 cup (160g) pure icing (confectioners') sugar
food colourings

1 Preheat oven to 180°C/350°F. Grease oven trays.
2 Combine butter, sugar and golden syrup in a small microwave-safe bowl; microwave, uncovered, on HIGH (100%) about 1 minute or until butter melts. Cool 5 minutes.
3 Sift combined flour, spices and soda into a large bowl; stir in butter mixture, egg and extract.
4 Divide dough in half; knead each portion of dough on floured surface. Roll dough between sheets of baking paper until 5mm (¼ inch) thick. Using gingerbread-people cutters, cut out shapes; place on oven trays.
5 Bake gingerbread about 10 minutes; cool on trays.
6 Make royal icing.
7 Decorate gingerbread people with icing.

ROYAL ICING

Beat egg white in a small bowl with an electric mixer until just frothy; gradually add sifted icing sugar, beating between additions, until stiff peaks form. Tint as desired with various food colourings.

If the mixture in step 3 is dry and crumbly, add a little more beaten egg – enough to make it feel like play dough.
To make a quick piping bag, snip the corner off a small plastic bag.
You obviously need a gingerbread-man cutter to make this shape, but any decorative cutter – a star, diamond, heart or whatever shape you may already have in your kitchen – can be used for this recipe.
Gingerbread people will keep in an airtight container for at least a week.

DECORATING SUGGESTIONS

You could also use coloured cachous or mini smarties to make buttons or other patterns.

PINEAPPLE AND COCONUT
Slice

PREP + COOK TIME *1 HOUR 10 MINUTES* MAKES *16*

150g (4½ ounces) butter, softened
⅔ cup (150g) caster (superfine) sugar
2 eggs
1½ cups (225g) plain (all-purpose) flour
¼ cup (35g) self-raising flour
¾ cup (180g) sour cream
2 tablespoons milk
440g (14 ounces) canned pineapple slices
   in natural juice

COCONUT CRUMBLE
½ cup (75g) plain (all-purpose) flour
¼ cup (55g) firmly packed light brown sugar
50g (1½ ounces) cold butter, chopped coarsely
½ cup (25g) flaked coconut

1 Preheat oven to 180°C/350°F. Grease a 20cm x 30cm (8-inch x 12-inch) rectangular pan; line base and long sides with baking paper, extending the paper 5cm (2 inches) over sides.

2 Make coconut crumble.

3 Beat butter and sugar in a small bowl with an electric mixer until light and fluffy. Beat in eggs, one at a time. Fold in sifted flours, sour cream and milk. Spread mixture into pan.

4 Meanwhile, drain pineapple well; discard juice (or reserve for another use). Cut slices in half horizontally, then in half crossways.

5 Arrange pineapple slices on mixture in pan; sprinkle with coconut crumble.

6 Bake slice about 45 minutes. Stand slice in pan for 10 minutes; transfer to a wire rack to cool.

COCONUT CRUMBLE
Combine sifted flour and sugar in a small bowl; rub in butter. Stir in coconut.

This slice will keep in an airtight container in the fridge for up to three days.

SERVING SUGGESTION
Serve warm with whipped cream.

MARMALADE GINGER
and Almond Slice

MARMALADE, GINGER
and *Almond Slice*

PREP + COOK TIME *1 HOUR* MAKES *24*

90g (3 ounces) unsalted butter, softened
½ cup (110g) caster (superfine) sugar
1 egg
⅔ cup (100g) plain (all-purpose) flour
⅓ cup (50g) self-raising flour
1 cup (340g) orange marmalade
⅓ cup (60g) finely chopped glacé ginger
1 egg, beaten lightly, extra
1½ cups (120g) flaked almonds
½ cup (60g) ground almonds
1 tablespoon icing (confectioners') sugar

1 Preheat oven to 160°C/325°F. Grease a 20cm x 30cm
   (8-inch x 12-inch) rectangular pan; line base and
   long sides with baking paper, extending the paper
   5cm (2 inches) over sides.
2 Beat butter, caster sugar and egg in a small bowl
   with an electric mixer until light and fluffy. Stir
   in sifted flours. Spread dough into pan. Combine
   marmalade and ginger in a small bowl; spread
   over dough.
3 Combine extra egg, 1 cup (80g) of the flaked
   almonds and ground almonds in a medium bowl.
   Spread almond mixture over marmalade; sprinkle
   with remaining nuts.
4 Bake slice about 40 minutes. Cool slice in pan.
   Dust with sifted icing sugar before cutting.

This slice will keep in an airtight container for
up to a week.

RASPBERRY WALNUT
Slice

PREP + COOK TIME *55 MINUTES* MAKES *20*

150g (4½ ounces) butter, softened
⅔ cup (110g) icing (confectioners') sugar
1¾ cups (260g) plain (all-purpose) flour
½ teaspoon ground cinnamon
½ cup (60g) ground walnuts
300g (9½ ounces) frozen raspberries

1 Preheat oven to 180°C/350°F. Grease a 20cm x 30cm
   (8-inch x 12-inch) rectangular pan; line base and
   long sides with baking paper, extending the paper
   5cm (2 inches) over sides.
2 Beat butter and sifted icing sugar in a medium
   bowl with an electric mixer until light and fluffy.
   Stir in sifted flour, cinnamon and nuts until mixture
   is crumbly.
3 Reserve 1 cup of crumble mixture. Press remaining
   mixture into pan; top with raspberries. Sprinkle
   with reserved crumble mixture.
4 Bake slice about 40 minutes. Cool slice in pan
   before cutting.

Walnut halves or pieces can be ground finely in
a blender or processor.
This slice will keep in an airtight container for
up to three days.

(PHOTOGRAPH PAGE 32)

RASPBERRY WALNUT
Slice
(RECIPE PAGE 31)

CHOCOLATE
Caramel Slice

(RECIPE PAGE 34)

CHOCOLATE
Caramel Slice

PREP + COOK TIME *55 MINUTES (+ REFRIGERATION)* **MAKES** *48*

1 cup (150g) plain (all-purpose) flour
½ cup (110g) firmly packed light brown sugar
½ cup (40g) desiccated coconut
125g (4 ounces) butter, melted
60g (2 ounces) butter, extra
395g (12½ ounces) canned sweetened
  condensed milk
2 tablespoons golden syrup or treacle
185g (6 ounces) dark eating (semi-sweet)
  chocolate, chopped coarsely
2 teaspoons vegetable oil

1 Preheat oven to 180°C/350°F. Grease a 20cm x 30cm
  (8-inch x 12-inch) rectangular pan; line base and
  long sides with baking paper, extending the paper
  5cm (2 inches) over sides.
2 Combine sifted flour, sugar and coconut in a
  medium bowl; stir in butter. Press mixture firmly
  over base of pan; bake about 15 minutes. Cool.
3 Place extra butter, condensed milk and syrup in a
  medium saucepan; stir over low heat until smooth.
  Pour mixture over base. Bake about 15 minutes or
  until golden brown. Cool.
4 Stir chocolate and oil in a medium heatproof bowl
  over a medium saucepan of simmering water
  until smooth. Spread chocolate mixture over slice.
  Refrigerate about 30 minutes or until set before
  cutting with a hot knife.

This slice will keep in an airtight container for up
to a week. If the weather is hot, store the container
in the fridge.

(PHOTOGRAPH PAGE 33)

DATE AND ALMOND
Brownies

PREP + COOK TIME *1 HOUR 15 MINUTES (+ COOLING)* **MAKES** *24*

300g (9½ ounces) dark eating (semi-sweet)
  chocolate, chopped coarsely
200g (6½ ounces) butter, chopped coarsely
125g (4 ounces) fresh dates, seeded
4 eggs
¾ cup (165g) caster (superfine) sugar
1 cup (120g) ground almonds
⅔ cup (100g) plain (all-purpose) flour
1 tablespoon cocoa powder
2 tablespoons roasted flaked almonds

1 Preheat oven to 170°C/340°F. Grease a deep 22cm
  (9-inch) square cake pan; line base and sides with
  baking paper, extending the paper 5cm (2 inches)
  over sides.
2 Stir chocolate and butter in a medium saucepan
  over low heat until smooth. Stir in dates. Transfer
  mixture to a medium bowl; cool 10 minutes.
3 Whisk eggs and sugar into chocolate mixture, then
  stir in ground almonds and sifted flour and cocoa.
  Pour mixture into pan; sprinkle with nuts.
4 Bake brownies about 35 minutes. Cool brownies
  in pan before cutting. Dust with a little extra
  cocoa powder.

These brownies are very fudgy; refrigerate for
several hours to make cutting them easier.
Store brownies in an airtight container for up to
a week. If the weather is hot, store the container
in the fridge.

DATE AND ALMOND
Brownies

HONEY WALNUT
and Oat Squares

HONEY WALNUT
and Oat Squares

PREP + COOK TIME *40 MINUTES* **MAKES** *30*

1 cup (150g) self-raising flour
1 cup (220g) caster (superfine) sugar
1 cup (90g) rolled oats
1 cup (80g) desiccated coconut
⅔ cup (70g) coarsely chopped walnuts
2 eggs, beaten lightly
125g (4 ounces) unsalted butter, melted, cooled
1 tablespoon creamed honey
½ cup (55g) coarsely chopped walnuts,
    roasted, extra

HONEY ICING

1 cup (160g) icing (confectioners') sugar
45g (1½ ounces) unsalted butter, melted
1 teaspoon creamed honey
1 tablespoon hot water, approximately

1 Preheat oven to 160°C/325°F. Grease a 23cm x 32cm (9-inch x 13-inch) swiss roll pan; line base and long sides with baking paper, extending the paper 5cm (2 inches) over sides.
2 Combine sifted flour, sugar, oats, coconut and nuts in a large bowl. Stir in eggs, butter and honey. Press mixture firmly into pan. Bake about 25 minutes. Cool slice in pan.
3 Meanwhile, make honey icing.
4 Drizzle slice with icing; sprinkle with extra nuts. Let icing set at room temperature before cutting slice.

HONEY ICING

Combine sifted icing sugar in a small bowl with butter, honey and enough of the hot water to make icing pourable.

This slice will keep in an airtight container for up to a week.

COFFEE PECAN
Slice

PREP + COOK TIME *1 HOUR* **MAKES** *24*

125g (4 ounces) butter, softened
¼ cup (55g) caster (superfine) sugar
1 cup (150g) plain (all-purpose) flour
¼ cup (35g) self-raising flour
2 cups (280g) pecans, roasted

COFFEE TOPPING

2 teaspoons instant coffee granules
3 teaspoons boiling water
2 eggs
½ cup (175g) golden syrup or treacle
⅓ cup (75g) firmly packed light brown sugar
60g (2 ounces) butter, melted
2 tablespoons plain (all-purpose) flour

1 Preheat oven to 200°C/400°F. Grease a 20cm x 30cm (8-inch x 12-inch) rectangular pan; line base and long sides with baking paper, extending the paper 5cm (2 inches) over sides.
2 Beat butter and sugar in a small bowl with an electric mixer until light and fluffy. Stir in sifted flours, in two batches. Press dough over base of pan.
3 Bake 10 minutes; cool in pan 10 minutes. Reduce oven to 180°C/350°F.
4 Meanwhile, make coffee topping.
5 Pour topping over base; scatter nuts over topping, in a single layer. Bake slice about 25 minutes or until set. Cool slice in pan before cutting.

COFFEE TOPPING

Dissolve coffee in the boiling water in a medium heatproof bowl. Whisk in eggs, syrup, sugar, butter and flour until combined.

This slice will keep in an airtight container for up to a week.

(PHOTOGRAPH PAGE 40)

COFFEE PECAN
Slice

(RECIPE PAGE 39)

MOCHA HEDGEHOG
Slice

(RECIPE PAGE 42)

MOCHA HEDGEHOG
Slice

PREP + COOK TIME *20 MINUTES (+ STANDING & REFRIGERATION)*
MAKES *40*

⅓ cup (50g) raisins
¼ cup (60ml) hot strong coffee
400g (12½ ounces) dark eating (semi-sweet) chocolate, chopped coarsely
155g (5 ounces) butter, chopped coarsely
1 egg
¼ cup (55g) caster (superfine) sugar
185g (6 ounces) shortbread biscuits, chopped coarsely
1 cup (140g) unsalted macadamias, roasted, chopped coarsely

1 Combine raisins and coffee in a small bowl; stand 1 hour.
2 Grease a 20cm x 30cm (8-inch x 12-inch) rectangular pan; line base and long sides with baking paper, extending the paper 5cm (2 inches) over sides.
3 Stir chocolate and butter in a medium heatproof bowl over a medium saucepan of simmering water until smooth.
4 Beat egg and sugar in a small bowl with an electric mixer until thick and doubled in volume. Stir into chocolate mixture. Fold coffee mixture and remaining ingredients into egg mixture.
5 Spread mixture into pan. Cover surface with plastic wrap, smooth surface with spatula or hands. Refrigerate 3 hours or overnight before cutting into pieces.

This slice will keep in an airtight container in the refrigerator for up to a week. Serve straight from the fridge.

(PHOTOGRAPH PAGE 41)

CHOCOLATE
Wheaties

PREP + COOK TIME *50 MINUTES (+ REFRIGERATION & STANDING)*
MAKES *18*

90g (3 ounces) butter, softened
½ cup (110g) firmly packed light brown sugar
1 egg
¼ cup (20g) desiccated coconut
⅓ cup (35g) wheat germ
⅔ cup (100g) wholemeal plain (all-purpose) flour
⅓ cup (50g) white self-raising flour
185g (6 ounces) dark eating (semi-sweet) chocolate, chopped coarsely

1 Beat butter and sugar in a small bowl with an electric mixer until smooth. Beat in egg until combined. Stir in coconut, wheat germ and sifted flours.
2 Roll dough between sheets of baking paper until 5mm (¼ inch) thick. Place on tray; refrigerate 30 minutes.
3 Preheat oven to 180°C/350°F. Line oven trays with baking paper.
4 Cut 7.5cm (3-inch) rounds from dough; place rounds about 2.5cm (1 inch) apart on trays.
5 Bake biscuits about 20 minutes. Cool on trays.
6 Meanwhile, stir chocolate in a small heatproof bowl over a small saucepan of simmering water until melted. Cool.
7 Spread bases of wheaties with chocolate; mark with a fork. Stand at room temperature until set.

If the weather is cool, store these biscuits in an airtight container at room temperature – if it's hot, keep the container in the fridge.

CHOCOLATE
Wheaties

DATE AND LEMON
Slice

PREP + COOK TIME *1 HOUR 10 MINUTES (+ COOLING)* **MAKES** *16*

1⅔ cups (250g) plain (all-purpose) flour
150g (4½ ounces) cold butter, chopped coarsely
1 egg, beaten lightly
1 teaspoon vanilla extract
1 teaspoon finely grated lemon rind
¾ cup (165g) caster (superfine) sugar
¾ cup (60g) desiccated coconut
⅓ cup (40g) coarsely chopped walnuts
¼ cup (15g) shredded coconut

DATE FILLING

1½ cups (250g) seeded dried dates,
    chopped coarsely
½ cup (110g) caster (superfine) sugar
⅔ cup (160ml) water
⅓ cup (80ml) lemon juice

1   Make date filling.
2   Preheat oven to 180°C/350°F. Grease a 20cm x 30cm
    (8-inch x 12-inch) rectangular pan; line base and
    long sides with baking paper, extending the paper
    5cm (2 inches) over sides.
3   Sift flour into a large bowl; rub in butter. Stir in
    combined egg, extract and rind, then sugar,
    desiccated coconut and walnuts.
4   Press half the flour mixture firmly over base of pan.
    Spread filling over base. Add shredded coconut to
    remaining flour mixture then sprinkle over filling.
5   Bake slice about 35 minutes. Cool in pan before
    cutting into pieces.

DATE FILLING

Bring dates, sugar and the water to the boil in a
medium saucepan. Reduce heat; simmer, stirring,
about 3 minutes or until dates are pulpy. Stir in
juice; cool.

This slice will keep in an airtight container for
up to three days.

TANGY LEMON *Squares*

PREP + COOK TIME *50 MINUTES (+ COOLING)* **MAKES** *16*

125g (4 ounces) butter, softened
¼ cup (40g) icing (confectioners') sugar
1¼ cups (185g) plain (all-purpose) flour
3 eggs
1 cup (220g) caster (superfine) sugar
2 teaspoons finely grated lemon rind
½ cup (125ml) lemon juice

1 Preheat oven to 180°C/350°F. Grease a shallow 24cm (9½-inch) square cake pan; line base and sides with baking paper, extending the paper 5cm (2 inches) above sides.
2 Beat butter and sifted icing sugar in a small bowl with an electric mixer until smooth. Stir in 1 cup (150g) of the sifted flour. Press mixture evenly over the base of pan.
3 Bake about 15 minutes or until browned lightly.
4 Meanwhile, whisk eggs, caster sugar, remaining sifted flour, rind and juice in a medium bowl until combined. Pour egg mixture over hot base.
5 Bake slice about 20 minutes or until firm. Cool slice in pan on a wire rack before cutting into squares. Serve dusted with extra sifted icing sugar, if you like.

This recipe is also delicious made with orange or mandarin rind and juice.
These squares will keep in an airtight container in the fridge for up to three days.

HONEY AND COCONUT *Muesli Slice*

PREP + COOK TIME *50 MINUTES* **MAKES** *36*

2½ cups (225g) rolled oats
1 cup (35g) rice bubbles
½ cup (40g) shredded coconut
½ cup (70g) slivered almonds
1 tablespoon honey
395g (14 ounces) canned sweetened
   condensed milk

1 Preheat oven to 160°C/325°F. Grease a 23cm x 32cm (9-inch x 13-inch) swiss roll pan; line base and long sides with baking paper, extending the paper 5cm (2 inches) over sides.
2 Combine ingredients in a large bowl; press mixture firmly into pan.
3 Bake slice about 40 minutes or until browned lightly. Cool slice in pan before cutting into pieces.

This slice will keep in an airtight container for up to a week.

TANGY LEMON
Squares

HONEY AND COCONUT
Muesli Slice

GARIBALDI SLICE

PREP + COOK TIME *50 MINUTES (+ REFRIGERATION)* **MAKES** *24*

1½ cups (240g) dried currants
½ cup (80g) sultanas
½ cup (75g) raisins
½ cup (125ml) water
2 tablespoons dry sherry
1 egg, beaten lightly
2 tablespoons caster (superfine) sugar

PASTRY
2 cups (300g) plain (all-purpose) flour
⅓ cup (75g) caster (superfine) sugar
185g (6 ounces) cold butter, chopped coarsely
2 egg yolks
1 tablespoon iced water, approximately

1 Preheat oven to 180°C/350°F. Grease a 23cm x 32cm (9-inch x 13-inch) swiss roll pan.
2 Make pastry.
3 Combine fruit, the water and sherry in a small saucepan; stir over low heat for about 5 minutes or until liquid is absorbed and fruit is soft. Blend or process fruit mixture until smooth. Cool.
4 Roll one portion of pastry between sheets of baking paper until large enough to line base of pan; lift pastry into pan, trimming to fit. Spread fruit mixture over pastry. Roll remaining pastry until large enough to cover fruit; lift pastry over fruit mixture, trimming to fit. Press down firmly. Cut top layer of pastry into 24 rectangles; prick each rectangle all over with a fork. Brush pastry with egg; sprinkle with sugar.
5 Bake slice about 30 minutes. Cool slice in pan before cutting into pieces.

PASTRY
Sift flour and sugar into a medium bowl; rub in butter. Stir in egg yolks and enough of the water to make a firm dough. Knead dough on floured surface until smooth. Divide dough in half; enclose each in plastic wrap, refrigerate 30 minutes.

This slice will keep in an airtight container for up to three days.

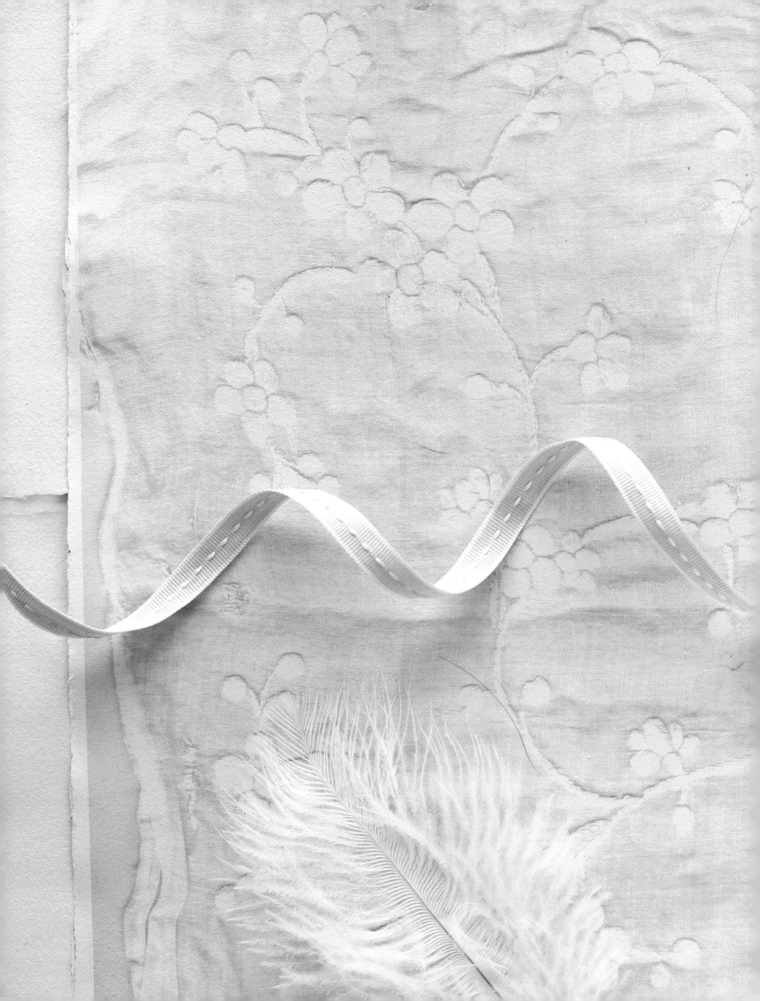

CHAPTER 2
TEACAKES
& PIKELETS

BUTTERSCOTCH TEACAKES
with Roasted Rhubarb

PREP + COOK TIME *1 HOUR 20 MINUTES* MAKES *8*

125g (4 ounces) butter, softened
1 teaspoon vanilla extract
¾ cup (165g) firmly packed dark brown sugar
2 eggs
¾ cup (110g) self-raising flour
¾ cup (110g) plain (all-purpose) flour
⅔ cup (160ml) milk
10g (½ ounce) butter, melted
1 tablespoon dark brown sugar, extra
½ teaspoon mixed spice

ROASTED RHUBARB

500g (1 pound) rhubarb, trimmed
30g (1 ounce) butter, melted
2 tablespoons caster (superfine) sugar

1 Preheat oven to 180°C/350°F.
2 Make roasted rhubarb.
3 Grease an 8-hole (¾-cup/180ml) mini loaf pan; line base and sides with baking paper.
4 Beat softened butter, extract and sugar in a small bowl with an electric mixer until light and fluffy. Beat in eggs, one at a time. Transfer mixture to a large bowl; stir in sifted flours and milk, in two batches. Spoon mixture into pan holes.
5 Bake teacakes about 25 minutes. Stand in pan 5 minutes; turn, top-side up, onto a wire rack.
6 Brush top of hot teacakes with melted butter; sprinkle with combined extra sugar and spice. Serve teacakes warm, topped with rhubarb.

ROASTED RHUBARB

Cut rhubarb into 6cm (2-inch) lengths. Place rhubarb in a small shallow baking dish with butter and sugar; toss to combine. Bake about 30 minutes or until rhubarb is tender but still holds its shape.

These teacakes are best served warm.

APPLE CUSTARD
Teacake

PREP + COOK TIME *2 HOURS (+ COOLING)* **SERVES** *8*

200g (6½ ounces) butter, softened
½ cup (110g) caster (superfine) sugar
2 eggs
1¼ cups (185g) self-raising flour
⅓ cup (40g) custard powder
2 medium green-skinned apples (300g),
    peeled, cored, sliced thinly
1 tablespoon butter, melted
2 teaspoons caster (superfine) sugar, extra
½ teaspoon ground cinnamon

CUSTARD

2 tablespoons custard powder
¼ cup (55g) caster (superfine) sugar
1 cup (250ml) milk
20g (¾ ounce) butter
2 teaspoons vanilla extract

1. Make custard.
2. Preheat oven to 180°C/350°F. Grease a deep 22cm (9-inch) round cake pan; line base with baking paper.
3. Beat butter and sugar in a small bowl with an electric mixer until light and fluffy. Beat in eggs, one at a time. Stir in sifted flour and custard powder.
4. Spread half the mixture into the pan, top with custard. Top custard with spoonfuls of remaining teacake mixture; gently spread with a spatula to completely cover custard. Arrange apples on top; brush with melted butter, then sprinkle with combined extra sugar and cinnamon.
5. Bake teacake about 1¼ hours; cool in pan. Sprinkle with extra caster sugar, if you like.

CUSTARD

Combine custard powder and sugar in a small saucepan; gradually add milk, stirring over heat until mixture thickens slightly. Remove from heat; stir in butter and extract. Transfer to a small bowl, cover surface with plastic wrap to prevent a skin forming; cool. Whisk until smooth just before using.

This teacake is best eaten the day it is made.

CINNAMON TEACAKE

PREP + COOK TIME *45 MINUTES* SERVES *10*

60g (2 ounces) butter, softened
⅔ cup (150g) caster (superfine) sugar
1 teaspoon vanilla extract
1 egg
1 cup (150g) self-raising flour
⅓ cup (80ml) milk
15g (½ ounce) butter, melted, extra
1 teaspoon ground cinnamon
1 tablespoon caster (superfine) sugar, extra

1 Preheat oven to 180°C/350°F. Grease a deep 20cm (8-inch) round cake pan; line base with baking paper.
2 Beat butter, sugar, extract and egg in a small bowl with an electric mixer until light and fluffy. Stir in sifted flour and milk. Spread mixture into pan.
3 Bake teacake about 30 minutes. Stand in pan 5 minutes; turn, top-side up, onto a wire rack.
4 Brush top of hot teacake with extra butter, sprinkle with combined cinnamon and extra sugar.

To make a light, fluffy teacake, it is important to cream the butter, sugar, vanilla extract and egg until the mixture is as light and as white as possible. This teacake is best eaten warm from the oven.

SERVING SUGGESTION
Serve warm with butter.

MADEIRA CAKE

PREP + COOK TIME *1 HOUR 15 MINUTES* SERVES *12*

185g (6 ounces) butter, softened
2 teaspoons finely grated lemon rind
⅔ cup (150g) caster (superfine) sugar
3 eggs
¾ cup (110g) plain (all-purpose) flour
¾ cup (110g) self-raising flour
⅓ cup (55g) mixed peel
¼ cup (35g) slivered almonds

1 Preheat oven to 160°C/325°F. Grease a deep 20cm (8-inch) round cake pan; line base with baking paper.
2 Beat butter, rind and sugar in small bowl with an electric mixer until light and fluffy; beat in eggs, one at a time. Transfer mixture to a large bowl; stir in sifted flours. Spread mixture into pan; sprinkle with peel and nuts.
3 Bake cake about 1 hour. Stand in pan 5 minutes; turn, top-side up, onto wire rack to cool.

This cake will keep in an airtight container, at room temperature, for up to four days. It can be frozen for up to two months.
This cake does not actually contain the sweet wine called Madeira. Its name is derived from the fact that it used to be served with a small glass of Madeira for afternoon – or high – tea in Victorian England.

(PHOTOGRAPH PAGE 58)

MADEIRA CAKE

(RECIPE PAGE 57)

ALMOND, LEMON AND PINE NUT
Teacake

(RECIPE PAGE 60)

ALMOND, LEMON AND PINE NUT
Teacake

PREP + COOK TIME *45 MINUTES* SERVES *8*

125g (4 ounces) butter, softened
½ cup (110g) caster (superfine) sugar
3 eggs
1 tablespoon finely grated lemon rind
2 tablespoons milk
1 cup (120g) ground almonds
¼ cup (35g) self-raising flour
2 tablespoons pine nuts
1 tablespoon flaked almonds

1   Preheat oven to 180°C/350°F. Grease a shallow
    13.5cm x 24cm (5½-inch x 9½-inch) loaf pan;
    line base with baking paper.
2   Beat butter, sugar, eggs and rind in a small bowl
    with an electric mixer until light and fluffy.
    Stir in milk, ground almonds and sifted flour.
    Spread mixture into pan; smooth surface.
    Sprinkle with nuts.
3   Bake teacake about 35 minutes. Stand in pan
    5 minutes; turn, top-side up, onto a wire rack
    to cool. Serve warm or at room temperature.

This teacake is best eaten the day it is made.

(PHOTOGRAPH PAGE 59)

CARAMELISED PINEAPPLE
and Coconut Teacakes

PREP + COOK TIME *50 MINUTES* MAKES *6*

60g (2 ounces) butter, softened
2 teaspoons coconut essence
⅓ cup (75g) caster (superfine) sugar
1 egg
⅔ cup (100g) self-raising flour
¼ cup (35g) plain (all-purpose) flour
¼ cup (20g) desiccated coconut
½ cup (125ml) milk
CARAMELISED PINEAPPLE
225g (7 ounces) canned pineapple slices
    in natural juice, drained
75g (2½ ounces) butter
⅓ cup (75g) firmly packed light brown sugar

1   Make caramelised pineapple.
2   Preheat oven to 180°C/350°F. Grease a 6-hole
    (¾-cup/180ml) texas muffin pan; line base of pan
    holes with rounds of baking paper.
3   Place one slice of caramelised pineapple in each
    pan hole; spoon half the caramel over pineapple.
4   Beat butter, essence, sugar and egg in a small bowl
    with an electric mixer until light and fluffy. Stir in
    sifted flours, coconut and milk. Spoon mixture into
    pan holes, smooth surface.
5   Bake teacakes about 25 minutes. Stand in pan
    5 minutes; turn, pineapple-side up, onto serving plates.
    Serve warm teacakes with any remaining syrup.

CARAMELISED PINEAPPLE
Slice pineapple rings in half horizontally. Stir butter
and sugar in a large frying pan over low heat until
sugar dissolves; bring to the boil. Add pineapple; cook,
turning occasionally, 3 minutes or until browned.

CARAMELISED PINEAPPLE
and Coconut Teacakes

SPICES OF THE ORIENT
Teacake

PREP + COOK TIME *45 MINUTES* SERVES *10*

60g (2 ounces) butter, softened
1 teaspoon vanilla extract
½ cup (110g) caster (superfine) sugar
1 egg
1 cup (150g) self-raising flour
⅓ cup (80ml) milk
20g (¾ ounce) butter, melted, extra

SPICED NUTS
2 tablespoons shelled pistachios,
    chopped finely
2 tablespoons blanched almonds,
    chopped finely
2 tablespoons pine nuts, chopped finely
¼ cup (40g) icing (confectioners') sugar
1 teaspoon ground cinnamon
½ teaspoon ground allspice
½ teaspoon ground cardamom

1 Preheat oven to 180°C/350°F. Grease a 20cm
   (8-inch) round cake pan.
2 Beat butter, extract, sugar and egg in a small bowl
   with an electric mixer until light and fluffy. Stir
   in sifted flour and milk. Spread mixture into pan.
3 Bake teacake about 25 minutes. Stand in pan
   5 minutes; turn, top-side up, onto a wire rack
   to cool.
4 Meanwhile, make spiced nuts.
5 Brush cooled teacake with extra butter; sprinkle
   with spiced nuts. Serve warm.

SPICED NUTS
Place nuts in a strainer; rinse under cold water.
Combine wet nuts in a large bowl with icing sugar
and spices; spread mixture onto an oven tray, roast
in oven about 10 minutes or until nuts are dry.

This teacake is best eaten the day it is made.

POACHED PEAR
and Nutmeg Teacake

PREP + COOK TIME 1 HOUR 30 MINUTES SERVES 10

200g (6½ ounces) butter, softened
¾ cup (150g) caster (superfine) sugar
2 teaspoons vanilla extract
2 eggs
2 cups (300g) self-raising flour
⅔ cup (160ml) buttermilk
30g (1 ounce) butter, melted
1 tablespoon caster (superfine) sugar, extra
½ teaspoon ground cinnamon
½ teaspoon ground nutmeg

POACHED PEARS
4 medium beurre bosc pears (950g)
1 cup (220g) caster (superfine) sugar
2 cups (500ml) dry white wine
2 cups (500ml) water
1 medium lemon (140g), halved
2 dried bay leaves

1 Make poached pears.
2 Preheat oven to 180°C/350°F. Grease a deep 22cm (9-inch) round cake pan; line base and side with baking paper.
3 Arrange poached pears on base of pan, rounded-side down.
4 Beat butter, sugar and extract in a small bowl with an electric mixer until light and fluffy. Beat in eggs, one at a time. Stir in sifted flour and buttermilk, in two batches. Spread mixture over pears in pan.
5 Bake teacake about 1 hour 10 minutes. Stand in pan 10 minutes; turn onto a wire rack.
6 Brush pears with melted butter; sprinkle with combined extra sugar and spices. Serve teacake warm with syrup.

POACHED PEARS
Peel, quarter and core pears. Place pears in a large saucepan with sugar, wine, the water, lemon and bay leaves; bring to the boil. Reduce heat; simmer, covered, about 25 minutes or until pears are tender. Using a slotted spoon, remove pears from syrup; cool. Remove and discard lemon halves; simmer remaining syrup, uncovered, over low heat, about 20 minutes until reduced.

This teacake is best eaten the day it is made.

SERVING SUGGESTION
Serve with whipped cream.

LEMON TEACAKES

PREP + COOK TIME *45 MINUTES* **MAKES** *8*

100g (3 ounces) butter, softened
⅓ cup (75g) caster (superfine) sugar
2 teaspoons finely grated lemon rind
1 egg
1 cup (150g) self-raising flour
⅓ cup (80ml) buttermilk
2 tablespoons lemon juice
20g (¾ ounce) butter, melted
LEMON SUGAR
½ cup (110g) white (granulated) sugar
5 x 5cm (2-inch) strips lemon rind

1 Preheat oven to 180°C/350°F. Grease eight holes
   of a 12-hole (⅓-cup/80ml) muffin pan well.
2 Beat softened butter, sugar, rind and egg in a
   small bowl with an electric mixer until light
   and fluffy. Stir in sifted flour, buttermilk and juice.
   Spoon mixture into pan holes; smooth surface.
3 Bake teacakes about 25 minutes. Stand in pan
   10 minutes; turn, top-side up, onto a wire rack.
4 Meanwhile, make lemon sugar.
5 Brush warm teacakes with melted butter; sprinkle
   with reserved lemon sugar. Serve warm.

LEMON SUGAR
Blend or process ingredients until fine. Reserve
2 tablespoons for this recipe; store the unused
sugar in an airtight container for another use.

These teacakes are best eaten the day they
are made.

CHERRY TEACAKE
with Vanilla Sugar

PREP + COOK TIME *1 HOUR 20 MINUTES* **SERVES** *10*

200g (6½ ounces) butter, softened
¾ cup (150g) firmly packed light brown sugar
2 teaspoons vanilla extract
2 eggs
2 cups (300g) self-raising flour
⅔ cup (160ml) buttermilk
425g (13½ ounces) canned pitted black
   cherries in syrup, drained
30g (1 ounce) butter, melted
VANILLA SUGAR
1 vanilla bean
½ cup (110g) white (granulated) sugar

1 Preheat oven to 180°C/350°F. Grease a deep 22cm
   (9-inch) round cake pan; line base and side with
   baking paper.
2 Beat softened butter, sugar and extract in a small
   bowl with an electric mixer until light and fluffy.
   Beat in eggs, one at a time. Stir in sifted flour and
   buttermilk, in two batches. Spread mixture into
   pan; top with cherries.
3 Bake teacake about 1 hour. Stand in pan 10 minutes;
   turn, top-side up, onto a wire rack.
4 Meanwhile, make vanilla sugar.
5 Brush warm teacake with melted butter; sprinkle
   with reserved vanilla sugar. Serve warm.

VANILLA SUGAR
Split vanilla bean in half lengthways; scrape seeds
into blender or processor. Add sugar; process until
fine. Reserve 2 tablespoons for this recipe; store
unused sugar in an airtight container for another use.

This teacake is best eaten the day it is made.

(PHOTOGRAPH PAGE 68)

CHERRY TEACAKE
with Vanilla Sugar
(RECIPE PAGE 67)

RASPBERRY PIKELETS
with Crème Fraîche

(RECIPE PAGE 70)

RASPBERRY PIKELETS
with Crème Fraîche

PREP + COOK TIME *45 MINUTES* **MAKES** *30*

1 cup (150g) self-raising flour
1 tablespoon caster (superfine) sugar
1 egg
1¼ cups (310ml) buttermilk
25g (¾ ounce) unsalted butter, melted
½ cup (70g) fresh raspberries, chopped
cooking-oil spray
½ cup (120g) crème fraîche
½ cup (70g) fresh raspberries, extra

1 Sift flour and sugar into a medium bowl. Whisk egg, buttermilk and butter in a medium jug. Gradually whisk egg mixture into flour mixture until smooth. Stir in chopped raspberries. Transfer batter to a large jug.

2 Spray a heated large heavy-based frying pan with cooking oil. Pour 1 tablespoon of batter for each pikelet into pan. Cook pikelets until bubbles appear on the surface; turn, brown other side. Remove from pan. Repeat with remaining batter.

3 Serve pikelets topped with crème fraîche and extra raspberries.

(PHOTOGRAPH PAGE 69)

PIKELETS WITH
Vanilla Blueberries and Cream

PREP + COOK TIME *30 MINUTES (+ REFRIGERATION)* **MAKES** *20*

1 cup (150g) self-raising flour
¼ cup (55g) caster (superfine) sugar
pinch bicarbonate of soda (baking soda)
1 egg
¾ cup (180ml) milk
1 teaspoon finely grated lemon rind
30g (1 ounce) butter
¾ cup (180ml) thick (double) cream

VANILLA BLUEBERRIES
1 vanilla bean
½ cup (110g) caster (superfine) sugar
½ cup (125ml) water
250g (8 ounces) blueberries

1 Make vanilla blueberries.

2 Sift flour, sugar and soda into a medium bowl. Make a well in centre; gradually whisk in combined egg, milk and rind.

3 Melt one-quarter of the butter in a large frying pan; drop level tablespoons of batter for each pikelet into pan. Cook pikelets until bubbles appear on surface; turn, brown other side. Remove from pan; cover to keep warm. Repeat with remaining butter and batter.

4 Serve pikelets with cream and vanilla blueberries.

VANILLA BLUEBERRIES
Split vanilla bean in half lengthways; scrape seeds into a medium saucepan. Add bean, sugar and the water; stir over low heat until sugar dissolves. Bring to the boil; boil, uncovered, 3 minutes. Stir in blueberries; simmer 1 minute. Cool 20 minutes. Cover; refrigerate 2 hours.

PIKELETS WITH
Vanilla Blueberries and Cream

BANOFFEE PIKELETS
with Cinnamon Cream

PREP + COOK TIME *45 MINUTES* MAKES *18*

1 cup (250ml) buttermilk
1 egg
½ cup mashed banana
1 cup (150g) self-raising flour
¼ teaspoon bicarbonate of soda (baking soda)
¼ cup (55g) firmly packed light brown sugar
40g (1½ ounces) butter
¾ cup (180ml) thickened (heavy) cream
¼ teaspoon ground cinnamon

CARAMEL SAUCE
½ cup (110g) caster (superfine) sugar
2 tablespoons water
½ cup (125ml) thickened (heavy) cream

1 Make caramel sauce.
2 Whisk buttermilk, egg and banana in a medium jug until combined. Sift flour and soda into a medium bowl, stir in sugar; gradually whisk in buttermilk mixture until smooth. Transfer mixture to a large jug.
3 Heat one-quarter of the butter in a large non-stick frying pan. Pour 2 tablespoons of batter for each pikelet into pan. Cook pikelets until bubbles appear on surface; turn, brown other side. Remove from pan; cover to keep warm. Repeat with remaining butter and batter.
4 Beat cream and cinnamon in a small bowl with an electric mixer until soft peaks form.
5 Serve pikelets with cream, drizzled with sauce.

CARAMEL SAUCE
Stir sugar and the water in a small saucepan over heat, without boiling, until sugar dissolves. Bring to the boil; boil, uncovered, without stirring, about 5 minutes or until golden brown. Remove from heat; carefully stir in cream (be careful, toffee may spatter). Cool.

You need one large overripe banana (230g) for the amount of mashed banana used in this recipe.

BLUEBERRY RICOTTA PIKELETS
with Caramelised Orange Sauce

PREP + COOK TIME *1 HOUR* **SERVES 6**

2 cups (300g) self-raising flour
¼ cup (55g) caster (superfine) sugar
2 eggs
1 cup (240g) smooth ricotta cheese
1¼ cup (310ml) buttermilk
2 teaspoons finely grated orange rind
125g (4 ounces) fresh blueberries
cooking-oil spray

CARAMELISED ORANGE SAUCE
5 medium oranges (1.2kg)
¾ cup (165g) caster (superfine) sugar
¾ cup (180ml) water

1 Sift flour and sugar into a large bowl. Whisk eggs, ricotta, buttermilk and rind in a large jug until combined. Gradually whisk egg mixture into flour mixture until smooth; stir in berries. Transfer batter to a large jug.

2 Spray a heated large heavy-based frying pan with cooking oil. Pour 1 tablespoon batter for each pikelet into pan. Cook pikelets until bubbles appear on surface; turn, brown other side. Remove from pan; cover to keep warm. Repeat with remaining batter.

3 Make caramelised orange sauce.

4 Serve pikelets with caramelised orange sauce.

CARAMELISED ORANGE SAUCE
Segment 4 of the oranges over a small bowl; squeeze membrane to release the juice, reserve. Squeeze juice from remaining orange; add to reserved juice. You need ¾ cup of juice in total. Stir sugar and the water in a medium saucepan over heat, without boiling, until sugar dissolves. Bring to the boil; boil, uncovered, about 10 minutes or until caramel in colour. Remove from heat, carefully stir in juice (be careful, toffee may spatter); stir over heat until all toffee pieces are dissolved. Stir in orange segments.

FRUIT MINCE
Pikelets

PREP + COOK TIME *30 MINUTES* **MAKES** *20*

1 cup (150g) self-raising flour
¼ teaspoon mixed spice
¼ cup (55g) firmly packed light brown sugar
pinch bicarbonate of soda (baking soda)
¾ cup (180ml) milk
1 egg
30g (1 ounce) butter
¾ cup (280g) fruit mince
2 tablespoons brandy

CUSTARD CREAM
2 tablespoons custard powder
2 tablespoons caster (superfine) sugar
1 cup (250ml) pouring cream
1 cup (250ml) thickened (heavy) cream

1   Make custard cream.
2   Sift flour, mixed spice, sugar and soda into a medium bowl. Make a well in centre; gradually whisk in combined milk and egg.
3   Melt one-quarter of the butter in a large frying pan; drop level tablespoons of batter for each pikelet into pan. Cook pikelets until bubbles appear on surface; turn, brown other side. Remove from pan; cover to keep warm. Repeat with remaining butter and batter.
4   Meanwhile, stir fruit mince and brandy in a small saucepan over heat until combined.
5   Serve pikelets with fruit mince mixture and custard cream.

CUSTARD CREAM
Blend custard powder and sugar with pouring cream in a small saucepan; stir over heat until mixture boils and thickens. Remove from heat; cover surface with plastic wrap. Cool 20 minutes. Beat thickened cream in a small bowl with an electric mixer until soft peaks form. Whisk cold custard in a small bowl until smooth; fold in cream.

CHAPTER 3
CAKES
& SPONGES

ORANGE AND PASSIONFRUIT CAKE
with Passionfruit Icing

PREP + COOK TIME *1 HOUR 20 MINUTES* **SERVES 12**

1 large orange (300g)
¼ cup (60ml) passionfruit pulp
185g (6 ounces) butter, softened
1 cup (220g) raw caster (superfine) sugar
2 eggs
2½ cups (375g) self-raising flour
¼ cup (60ml) milk

PASSIONFRUIT ICING

1½ cups (240g) icing (confectioners') sugar
10g (½ ounce) butter, softened
2 tablespoons passionfruit pulp, approximately

1 Preheat oven to 170°C/340°F. Grease a deep 14cm x 21cm (5½-inch x 8½-inch) loaf pan; line base and sides with baking paper, extending the paper 5cm (2 inches) over sides.

2 Using a vegetable peeler, remove rind from orange; reserve rind. Using small sharp knife, remove white pith from orange; discard pith. Quarter orange; discard seeds. Blend or process orange flesh and rind until pulpy. Stir in passionfruit pulp.

3 Beat butter, sugar, eggs, sifted flour, milk and orange mixture in a large bowl with an electric mixer on low speed until combined. Increase speed to high; beat about 2 minutes or until paler in colour. Spread mixture into pan.

4 Bake cake about 1 hour 10 minutes. Stand in pan 10 minutes; turn, top-side up, onto a wire rack over an oven tray to cool.

5 Meanwhile, make passionfruit icing.

6 Spread icing over cooled cake.

PASSIONFRUIT ICING
Stir ingredients in a medium bowl until mixture is smooth.

This cake will keep in an airtight container for up to three days. Uniced, this cake can be frozen for up to three months.

PISTACHIO AND ROSEWATER
Layer Cake

PREP + COOK TIME *2 HOURS (+ COOLING)* SERVES *12*

200g (6½ ounces) roasted unsalted
    shelled pistachios
250g (8 ounces) butter, softened
1½ cups (330g) caster (superfine) sugar
2 teaspoons finely grated lemon rind
4 eggs
1 cup (150g) plain (all-purpose) flour
½ cup (75g) self-raising flour
¾ cup (200g) Greek-style yogurt

ROSEWATER BUTTERCREAM
250g (8 ounces) butter, softened
2 teaspoons rosewater
3 cups (480g) icing (confectioners') sugar

1 Preheat oven to 170°C/340°F. Grease a deep 22cm (9-inch) round cake pan; line base and side with baking paper.
2 Blend or process nuts until finely ground.
3 Beat butter, sugar and rind in a medium bowl with an electric mixer until light and fluffy. Beat in eggs, one at a time. Stir in sifted flours, yogurt and 1 cup of the ground nuts. Spread mixture into pan.
4 Bake cake about 1 hour 10 minutes. Stand in pan 5 minutes; turn, top-side up, onto a wire rack to cool.
5 Make rosewater buttercream.
6 Split cooled cake in half. Place bottom layer, cut-side up, onto a serving plate; spread with one-third of the buttercream, top with remaining cake layer. Spread remaining buttercream all over cake. Sprinkle remaining ground nuts on top of cake.

ROSEWATER BUTTERCREAM
Beat butter and rosewater in a medium bowl with an electric mixer until as white as possible. Gradually beat in sifted icing sugar until smooth.

Rosewater will vary in strength between brands. Start adding a small amount at a time and adjust to your taste. If you're using rosewater essence, start with 1 teaspoon.
This cake will keep in an airtight container for up to three days.

LEMON CAKE WITH
Lemon Mascarpone Frosting

PREP + COOK TIME *1 HOUR 20 MINUTES (+ COOLING)* **SERVES** *8*

125g (4 ounces) butter, softened
2 teaspoons finely grated lemon rind
1¼ cups (275g) caster (superfine) sugar
3 eggs
1½ cups (225g) self-raising flour
½ cup (125ml) milk
¼ cup (60ml) lemon juice

LEMON MASCARPONE FROSTING

1 cup (250ml) thickened (heavy) cream
½ cup (80g) icing (confectioners') sugar
2 teaspoons finely grated lemon rind
⅔ cup (170g) mascarpone cheese

1 Preheat oven to 180°C/350°F. Grease a deep 20cm (8-inch) round cake pan; line base with baking paper.
2 Make lemon mascarpone frosting; refrigerate, covered, until required.
3 Beat butter, rind and sugar in a small bowl with an electric mixer until light and fluffy. Beat in eggs, one at a time (mixture might separate at this stage, but will come together later); transfer mixture to a large bowl. Stir in sifted flour, milk and juice, in two batches. Pour mixture into pan.
4 Bake cake about 50 minutes. Stand in pan 5 minutes; turn, top-side up, onto a wire rack to cool.
5 Split cold cake into three layers, place one layer onto a serving plate, cut-side up; spread with one-third of the frosting. Repeat layering process, finishing with frosting.

LEMON MASCARPONE FROSTING

Beat cream, sifted icing sugar and rind in a small bowl with an electric mixer until soft peaks form. Fold cream mixture into mascarpone.

Grate the lemon for the frosting before you extract the juice for the cake mixture.
This cake will keep in an airtight container, in the fridge, for up to three days.

COFFEE AND WALNUT *Cake*

PREP + COOK TIME *1 HOUR 15 MINUTES (+ COOLING & STANDING)* **SERVES** *8*

30g (1 ounce) butter
1 tablespoon light brown sugar
2 teaspoons ground cinnamon
2 cups (200g) roasted walnuts
½ cup (125ml) milk
1 tablespoon instant coffee granules
185g (6 ounces) butter, softened, extra
1⅓ cups (300g) caster (superfine) sugar
3 eggs
1 cup (150g) self-raising flour
¾ cup (110g) plain (all-purpose) flour

TOFFEE
½ cup (110g) caster (superfine) sugar
2 tablespoons water
3 teaspoons pouring cream

1 Preheat oven to 160°C/325°F. Butter a 22cm (9-inch) baba cake pan well; dust with flour, shake out excess.

2 Melt the butter in a small saucepan; stir in brown sugar, cinnamon and nuts. Cool.

3 Combine milk and coffee in a small bowl; stir until coffee dissolves.

4 Beat extra butter and caster sugar in a small bowl with an electric mixer until light and fluffy. Beat in eggs, one at a time. Stir in sifted flours, then milk mixture.

5 Spread one-third of the cake mixture into base of pan; sprinkle with half the nut mixture. Top with remaining cake mixture. Bake about 45 minutes. Stand in pan 5 minutes; turn onto a wire rack over an oven tray to cool.

6 Make toffee.

7 Working quickly, drizzle some of the toffee on top of cake, press on remaining walnut mixture; drizzle with remaining toffee.

TOFFEE
Stir sugar and the water in a small saucepan over heat, without boiling, until sugar dissolves; bring to the boil. Reduce heat; simmer, uncovered, until toffee becomes caramel in colour. Add cream; stir 1 minute or until thickened slightly.

This cake is best eaten the day it is made.

CARROT CAKE WITH
Lemon Cream Cheese Frosting

PREP + COOK TIME *1 HOUR 25 MINUTES* **SERVES** *12*

3 eggs
1⅓ cups (250g) firmly packed light brown sugar
1 cup (250ml) vegetable oil
3 cups coarsely grated carrot
1 cup (120g) coarsely chopped walnuts
2½ cups (375g) self-raising flour
½ teaspoon bicarbonate of soda (baking soda)
2 teaspoons mixed spice

LEMON CREAM CHEESE FROSTING
45g (1½ ounces) butter, softened
110g (3½ ounces) cream cheese, softened
1½ teaspoons finely grated lemon rind
2¼ cups (360g) icing (confectioners') sugar

1 Preheat oven to 180°C/350°F. Grease a deep 22cm (9-inch) round cake pan; line the base with baking paper.
2 Beat eggs, sugar and oil in a small bowl with an electric mixer until thick and creamy. Transfer mixture to a large bowl; stir in carrot and nuts, then sifted dry ingredients. Pour mixture into pan.
3 Bake cake about 1¼ hours. Stand in pan 5 minutes; turn, top-side up, onto a wire rack to cool.
4 Meanwhile, make lemon cream cheese frosting.
5 Split cold cake in half, place bottom layer onto a serving plate, cut-side up; spread with half the frosting. Top with remaining cake layer; spread top with remaining frosting.

LEMON CREAM CHEESE FROSTING
Beat butter, cream cheese and rind in a small bowl with an electric mixer until light and fluffy; gradually beat in sifted icing sugar.

You need three large carrots (540g) for the amount of grated carrot used in this recipe.
This cake will keep in an airtight container in the fridge for up to three days. Without the frosting, this cake can be frozen for up to three months.

BANANA AND CINNAMON

Muffins

PREP + COOK TIME 40 MINUTES MAKES 12

2 cups (300g) self-raising flour
⅓ cup (50g) plain (all-purpose) flour
1 teaspoon ground cinnamon
½ teaspoon bicarbonate of soda (baking soda)
½ cup (110g) firmly packed light brown sugar
1 cup mashed banana
2 eggs
¾ cup (180ml) buttermilk
⅓ cup (80ml) vegetable oil
½ teaspoon ground cinnamon, extra

CREAM CHEESE TOPPING
125g (4 ounces) cream cheese, softened
¼ cup (40g) icing (confectioners') sugar

1 Preheat oven to 200°C/400°F. Grease a 12-hole (⅓-cup/80ml) muffin pan.
2 Sift flours, cinnamon, soda and sugar into a large bowl; stir in banana, then combined eggs, buttermilk and oil. Spoon mixture into pan holes.
3 Bake muffins about 20 minutes. Stand in pan 5 minutes; turn, top-side up, onto a wire rack to cool.
4 Make cream cheese topping.
5 Spread cold muffins with topping; sprinkle with extra cinnamon.

CREAM CHEESE TOPPING
Beat ingredients in a small bowl with an electric mixer until smooth.

You need two large overripe bananas (460g) for the amount of mashed banana used in this recipe. Never throw away bruised or blackened bananas: just pop them in the freezer as they are, to have on hand whenever you want to make this recipe again. Overripe frozen bananas can also be thawed and mashed for use in making banana bread, pancakes or smoothies.
Muffins with the topping will keep in an airtight container, in the fridge, for up to three days. Plain muffins can be frozen for up to three months.

RASPBERRY AND ALMOND
Mascarpone Cake

PREP + COOK TIME *2 HOURS 45 MINUTES (+ STANDING & COOLING)* **SERVES** *25*

500g (1 pound) butter, softened
3 cups (660g) caster (superfine) sugar
8 eggs
2 cups (300g) plain (all-purpose) flour
1½ cups (225g) self-raising flour
1 cup (125g) ground almonds
1 cup (250ml) milk
1 cup (140g) roasted slivered almonds,
   chopped finely
400g (12½ ounces) fresh or frozen raspberries
400g (12½ ounces) vienna almonds

MASCARPONE CREAM

750g (1½ pounds) mascarpone cheese
1¼ cups (300g) sour cream
1 cup (160g) icing (confectioners') sugar
⅓ cup (80ml) orange-flavoured liqueur

1 Preheat oven to 160°C/325°F. Grease a deep 30cm (12-inch) round cake pan; line base and side with two layers of baking paper, extending the paper 5cm (2 inches) above side.
2 Beat butter and sugar in a large bowl with an electric mixer until light and fluffy. Beat in eggs, one at a time (mixture may separate at this stage, but will come together later).
3 Transfer mixture to a very large bowl; fold in sifted flours, ground almonds and milk, in three batches. Fold in chopped almonds and raspberries. Spread mixture into pan.
4 Bake cake 1 hour. Reduce oven to 150°C/300°F; bake about 1 hour. Stand in pan 20 minutes; turn, top-side up, onto a wire rack to cool.
5 Meanwhile, make mascarpone cream.
6 Using large serrated knife, split cake into three layers. Place base layer onto a serving plate; spread with one-third of the mascarpone cream, repeat layering, finishing with mascarpone cream. Decorate top of cake with vienna almonds.

MASCARPONE CREAM

Beat mascarpone, sour cream and sifted icing sugar in a large bowl with an electric mixer until soft peaks form; stir in liqueur.

Velvety mascarpone is sweet and slightly tart, like the raspberries it accompanies in this sumptuous, layered torte.
Unfilled cake will keep in an airtight container for up to two days. Split and fill the cake on day of serving. Unfilled cake can be frozen for up to three months.

BASIC BUTTER *Cake*

PREP + COOK TIME *1 HOUR 30 MINUTES* SERVES *12*

250g (8 ounces) butter, softened
1 teaspoon vanilla extract
1¼ cups (275g) caster (superfine) sugar
3 eggs
2¼ cups (335g) self-raising flour
¼ cup (35g) plain (all-purpose) flour
¾ cup (180ml) milk
2 teaspoons icing (confectioners') sugar

1 Preheat oven to 180°C/350°F. Grease a deep
   20cm (8-inch) square cake pan; line base and
   sides with baking paper.
2 Beat butter, extract and sugar in a medium
   bowl with an electric mixer until light and fluffy.
   Beat in eggs, one at a time. Stir in sifted flours and
   milk, in two batches. Spread mixture into pan;
   smooth surface.
3 Bake cake about 1 hour. Stand in pan 5 minutes;
   turn, top-side up, onto a wire rack to cool. Dust
   with sifted icing sugar before serving.

You can also use a 22cm (9-inch) round cake pan
for this recipe.
This cake will keep in an airtight container for up to
three days. It can be frozen for up to three months.

COCONUT AND *Lemon Syrup Cake*

PREP + COOK TIME *1 HOUR 10 MINUTES* SERVES *8*

125g (4 ounces) butter, softened
1 cup (220g) caster (superfine) sugar
4 eggs
2 cups (160g) desiccated coconut
1 cup (150g) self-raising flour
2 tablespoons desiccated coconut, extra
LEMON SYRUP
1 cup (220g) caster (superfine) sugar
1 cup (250ml) water
4 x 5cm (2-inch) strips lemon rind

1 Preheat oven to 160°C/325°F. Grease a deep
   20cm (8-inch) round cake pan; line base and
   side with baking paper.
2 Beat butter and sugar in a small bowl with an
   electric mixer until light and fluffy. Beat in eggs,
   one at a time. Transfer mixture to large bowl;
   stir in coconut and sifted flour. Spread mixture
   into pan; sprinkle with extra coconut.
3 Bake cake about 50 minutes.
4 Meanwhile, make lemon syrup.
5 Pour hot lemon syrup over hot cake in pan. Cool.

LEMON SYRUP
Stir ingredients in a small saucepan over heat,
without boiling, until sugar dissolves; bring to the
boil. Reduce heat; simmer, uncovered, without
stirring, 5 minutes. Strain.

This cake will keep in an airtight container for up
to three days.

(PHOTOGRAPH PAGE 96)

COCONUT AND
Lemon Syrup Cake
(RECIPE PAGE 95)

CARAMEL
Butter Cake
(RECIPE PAGE 98)

CARAMEL
Butter Cake

PREP + COOK TIME *1 HOUR 15 MINUTES* SERVES *10*

125g (4 ounces) butter, softened
1 cup (220g) firmly packed light brown sugar
1 teaspoon vanilla extract
2 eggs
1 tablespoon golden syrup or treacle
1 cup (150g) plain (all-purpose) flour
½ cup (75g) self-raising flour
1 teaspoon ground cinnamon
½ cup (125ml) milk

CARAMEL ICING
1 cup (220g) firmly packed light brown sugar
60g (2 ounces) butter
2 tablespoons milk
¾ cup (120g) icing (confectioners') sugar
2 teaspoons milk, extra

1 Preheat oven to 180°C/350°F. Grease a deep 20cm (8-inch) round cake pan; line base with baking paper.
2 Beat butter, sugar and extract in a small bowl with an electric mixer until light and fluffy. Beat in eggs and golden syrup. Stir in sifted flours and spices, and milk. Spread mixture into the pan.
3 Bake cake about 50 minutes. Stand in pan 5 minutes; turn, top-side up, onto a wire rack to cool.
4 Meanwhile, make caramel icing.
5 Spread icing on top of cold cake before serving.

CARAMEL ICING
Stir brown sugar, butter and milk in a small saucepan constantly, over heat without boiling until sugar dissolves. Bring to the boil. Reduce heat; simmer, uncovered, 3 minutes without stirring. Remove from heat; stir in sifted icing sugar. Stir in extra milk until icing is of a spreadable consistency.

This cake will keep in an airtight container for up to three days. Without the icing, it can be frozen for up to three months.

(PHOTOGRAPH PAGE 97)

MARSALA
and Fig Cake

PREP + COOK TIME *1 HOUR 45 MINUTES (+ COOLING)* SERVES *8*

250g (8 ounces) soft dried figs, chopped finely
½ cup (125ml) marsala
125g (4 ounces) butter, softened
1 cup (220g) firmly packed light brown sugar
2 eggs
1 cup (150g) self-raising flour
½ cup (75g) plain (all-purpose) flour
¼ teaspoon bicarbonate of soda (baking soda)
½ cup (140g) sour cream
1 tablespoon icing (confectioners') sugar

1 Preheat oven to 160°C/325°F. Grease a deep 22cm (9-inch) baba pan well.
2 Combine figs and marsala in a small saucepan; bring to the boil. Cool 15 minutes.
3 Meanwhile, beat butter and brown sugar in a small bowl with an electric mixer until light and fluffy. Beat in eggs, one at a time. Transfer mixture to a large bowl; stir in sifted flours and soda, and sour cream.
4 Blend or process fig mixture until it forms a smooth paste; stir into cake mixture. Spread mixture into the pan; smooth surface.
5 Bake cake about 1 hour. Stand in pan 5 minutes; turn onto a wire rack to cool. Dust with sifted icing sugar before serving.

This cake will keep in an airtight container for up to three days. It can be frozen for up to three months.

MARSALA AND FIG
Cake

CHOCOLATE AND
Roasted Almond Torte

PREP + COOK TIME *1 HOUR 15 MINUTES (+ COOLING)* SERVES *12*

1¼ cups (200g) blanched almonds, roasted
185g (6 ounces) butter, chopped coarsely
200g (6½ ounces) dark eating (semi-sweet)
    chocolate, chopped coarsely
6 eggs, separated
1 cup (220g) caster (superfine) sugar
1 cup (250g) thick (double) cream

ALMOND PRALINE
⅔ cup (50g) flaked almonds
1 cup (220g) caster (superfine) sugar
⅓ cup (80ml) water

CHOCOLATE GLAZE
½ cup (125ml) pouring cream
200g (6½ ounces) dark eating (semi-sweet)
    chocolate, chopped coarsely

1 Preheat oven to 180°C/350°F. Grease a 24cm
  (9½-inch) springform pan; line the base and side
  with baking paper.
2 Blend or process nuts until fine.
3 Stir butter and chocolate in a medium saucepan
  over low heat until smooth. Cool.
4 Beat egg yolks and sugar in a large bowl with an
  electric mixer until combined. Beat egg whites in
  a medium bowl with an electric mixer until soft
  peaks form.
5 Fold chocolate mixture and nuts into egg yolk
  mixture; fold in egg white mixture, in two batches.
  Pour mixture into pan.
6 Bake cake about 40 minutes. Stand in pan 10 minutes;
  transfer to a wire rack over an oven tray to cool.

7 Meanwhile, make almond praline and chocolate glaze.
8 Spread glaze over top and side of cake; sprinkle
  top with crushed praline. Serve cake with thick
  cream and praline shards.

ALMOND PRALINE
Preheat oven to 180°C/350°F. Place nuts on a
baking-paper-lined oven tray; roast about 5 minutes
or until browned lightly. Meanwhile, stir sugar and
the water in a small frying pan over heat without
boiling, until sugar dissolves; bring to the boil. Boil,
uncovered, without stirring, until mixture is caramel
in colour. Pour toffee over nuts on tray; stand at room
temperature until set. Break about one-third of the
praline into pieces; place in a resealable plastic bag,
seal tightly. Smash praline with a rolling pin or meat
mallet until crushed finely. Break remaining praline
into large shards.

CHOCOLATE GLAZE
Bring cream to the boil in a small saucepan.
Remove from heat; stir in chocolate until smooth.

This cake will keep in an airtight container for
up to three days.

SERVING SUGGESTION
Serve with vanilla ice-cream.

WHITE CHOCOLATE
Mud Cake

PREP + COOK TIME *2 HOURS 45 MINUTES (+ COOLING)* **SERVES** *12*

250g (8 ounces) butter, chopped coarsely
180g (5½ ounces) white eating chocolate,
  chopped coarsely
1½ cups (330g) caster (superfine) sugar
¾ cup (180ml) milk
1½ cups (225g) plain (all-purpose) flour
½ cup (75g) self-raising flour
½ teaspoon vanilla extract
2 eggs, beaten lightly

WHITE CHOCOLATE GANACHE

½ cup (125ml) thickened (heavy) cream
360g (11½ ounces) white eating chocolate,
  chopped finely

1 Preheat oven to 170°C/340°F. Grease deep 20cm (8-inch) round cake pan; line base and side with baking paper.
2 Stir butter, chocolate, sugar and milk in a medium saucepan over low heat until smooth. Transfer mixture to a large bowl; cool 15 minutes.
3 Whisk sifted flours, extract and egg into chocolate mixture; pour mixture into pan.
4 Bake cake about 1 hour 40 minutes; cool in pan.
5 Meanwhile, make white chocolate ganache.
6 Turn cake, top-side up, onto serving plate. Spread ganache all over cake.

WHITE CHOCOLATE GANACHE
Bring cream to the boil in a small saucepan; pour over chocolate in a medium heatproof bowl, stir until smooth. Cover; refrigerate, stirring occasionally, about 30 minutes or until spreadable.

This cake will keep in an airtight container, in the fridge, for up to a week. Without the ganache, it can be frozen for up to three months.

DARK CHOCOLATE
Mud Cake

PREP + COOK TIME *2 HOURS (+ COOLING)* **SERVES** *12*

250g (8 ounces) unsalted butter,
  chopped coarsely
2 cups (440g) caster (superfine) sugar
½ cup (125ml) milk
½ cup (125ml) strong black coffee
½ cup (125ml) bourbon
1 teaspoon vanilla extract
200g (6½ ounces) dark eating (semi-sweet)
  chocolate, chopped coarsely
1½ cups (225g) plain (all-purpose) flour
¼ cup (35g) self-raising flour
¼ cup (25g) cocoa powder
2 eggs

DARK CHOCOLATE GANACHE
½ cup (125ml) pouring cream
200g (6½ ounces) dark eating (semi-sweet)
  chocolate, chopped coarsely

1 Preheat oven to 160°C/325°F. Grease a deep 22cm (9-inch) square cake pan; line base and sides with baking paper.
2 Stir butter, sugar, milk, coffee, bourbon, extract and chocolate in a medium saucepan over low heat until smooth. Transfer mixture to a large bowl; cool 15 minutes.
3 Whisk in sifted flours and cocoa, then eggs. Pour mixture into pan.
4 Bake cake about 1½ hours. Stand in pan 5 minutes; turn, top-side up, onto a wire rack to cool.
5 Meanwhile, make dark chocolate ganache.
6 Spread ganache over cold cake.

DARK CHOCOLATE GANACHE
Bring cream to the boil in a small saucepan. Remove from heat, add chocolate; stir until smooth. Stand 10 minutes before using.

This cake will keep in an airtight container, in the fridge, for up to a week. Without the ganache, it can be frozen for up to three months.

BANANA CAKE
with Caramel Sauce

PREP + COOK TIME *1 HOUR 15 MINUTES* SERVES *10*

155g (5 ounces) butter, softened
¾ cup (165g) firmly packed light brown sugar
2 eggs
1½ cups mashed banana
1 teaspoon bicarbonate of soda (baking soda)
2 tablespoons hot milk
1 cup (150g) plain (all-purpose) flour
⅔ cup (100g) self-raising flour

CARAMEL SAUCE
50g (1½ ounces) butter
½ cup (110g) firmly packed light brown sugar
2 tablespoons golden syrup

1 Preheat oven to 180°C/350°F. Grease a deep 20cm (8-inch) round cake pan; line base and side with baking paper.

2 Beat butter and sugar in a small bowl with an electric mixer until light and fluffy. Beat in eggs, one at a time. Transfer mixture to a large bowl; stir in banana. Combine soda and milk in small jug; stir into banana mixture. Stir in sifted flours, in two batches. Spread mixture into pan.

3 Bake cake about 50 minutes. Stand in pan 5 minutes; turn, top-side up, onto a wire rack to cool.

4 Meanwhile, make caramel sauce.

5 Serve slices of cake drizzled with warm sauce.

CARAMEL SAUCE
Stir ingredients in a small saucepan over low heat until sugar is dissolved and mixture is smooth.

You need three large overripe bananas (690g) for the amount of mashed banana used in this recipe. The cake will keep in an airtight container, at room temperature, for up to four days. Store any unused sauce in the refrigerator. The cake can be frozen for up to three months.

CHOCOLATE VELVET
Cake

PREP + COOK TIME *1 HOUR 10 MINUTES (+ REFRIGERATION)* SERVES *16*

125g (4 ounces) butter, softened
1 cup (220g) firmly packed light brown sugar
½ cup (110g) caster (superfine) sugar
3 eggs
2 cups (300g) plain (all-purpose) flour
⅓ cup (35g) cocoa powder
1 teaspoon bicarbonate of soda (baking soda)
⅔ cup (160g) sour cream
½ cup (125ml) water

CHOCOLATE GLAZE

90g (3 ounces) dark eating (semi-sweet)
   chocolate, chopped coarsely
60g (2 ounces) butter, chopped coarsely
½ cup (80g) icing (confectioners') sugar
¼ cup (60g) sour cream

1 Preheat oven to 180°C/350°F. Grease a deep 23cm x 30cm (9-inch x 12-inch) rectangular cake pan or baking dish; line base and sides with baking paper, extending the paper 5cm (2 inches) above long sides.
2 Beat ingredients in a large bowl with an electric mixer on low speed until just combined. Increase speed to medium; beat about 3 minutes or until mixture is smooth and paler in colour. Spread mixture into pan.
3 Bake cake about 45 minutes. Stand in pan 10 minutes; turn, top-side up, onto a wire rack to cool.
4 Meanwhile, make chocolate glaze.
5 Spread cold cake with chocolate glaze; stand until set before cutting.

CHOCOLATE GLAZE

Stir ingredients in a small saucepan over low heat until smooth; cook, stirring, 2 minutes. Transfer to a small bowl; cool 10 minutes. Refrigerate about 20 minutes or until glaze is spreadable.

This cake will keep in an airtight container, at room temperature, for up to three days. Without the glaze, cake can be frozen for up to two months.

MUSCAT PRUNE
Shortcake

PREP + COOK TIME *55 MINUTES (+ COOLING & REFRIGERATION)* **SERVES** *12*

200g (6½ ounces) butter, softened
1 teaspoon finely grated lemon rind
⅓ cup (75g) caster (superfine) sugar
¼ cup (50g) rice flour
¾ cup (110g) plain (all-purpose) flour
¾ cup (110g) self-raising flour
1¼ cups (310ml) thickened (heavy) cream
   (see notes)
1 tablespoon caster (superfine) sugar, extra

MUSCAT PRUNES
1 cup (170g) seeded prunes, chopped coarsely
1 cup (250ml) muscat

1 Preheat oven to 180°C/350°F. Grease three 20cm (8-inch) round sandwich pans.
2 Beat butter, rind and sugar in a medium bowl with an electric mixer until light and fluffy. Fold in sifted flours, in two batches. Press mixture evenly into pans.
3 Bake shortcakes about 20 minutes. Cool in pans.
4 Meanwhile, make muscat prunes.
5 Beat cream in a small bowl with an electric mixer until firm peaks form. Place one shortcake into a deep 20cm (8-inch) round cake pan or 20cm (8-inch) springform tin; spread with half the prune mixture, then half the whipped cream. Top with another shortcake; spread with remaining prune mixture then remaining whipped cream. Top with remaining shortcake, cover; refrigerate overnight.
6 Remove shortcake from pan; serve sprinkled with extra sugar.

MUSCAT PRUNES
Stir prunes and muscat in a small saucepan over heat, without boiling, until prunes soften. Cool.

You can use just one 300ml carton of cream for this recipe.
A fortified wine, like sherry and port, muscat is the result of grapes left to ripen well beyond normal harvesting time, resulting in a concentrated dark, toffee-coloured wine with a rich yet mellow flavour. This cake is best made a day ahead and will keep in an airtight container, in the fridge, for up to three days.

COCONUT SPONGE
Cake

PREP + COOK TIME *45 MINUTES* SERVES *10*

185g (6 ounces) butter, chopped coarsely
¾ cup (165g) caster (superfine) sugar
3 eggs
⅔ cup (50g) desiccated coconut
1½ cups (225g) self-raising flour
1 teaspoon baking powder
⅓ cup (80ml) milk
2 teaspoons icing (confectioners') sugar

PASSIONFRUIT CREAM
1¼ cup (310ml) pouring cream (see note)
1 tablespoon caster (superfine) sugar
2 passionfruit

1   Preheat oven to 180°C/350°F. Grease a 20cm x 30cm (8-inch x 12-inch) rectangular pan; line base with baking paper.
2   Beat ingredients in a small bowl with an electric mixer on low speed until combined. Increase speed to medium, beat until mixture is smooth and has changed to a paler colour. Spread mixture into pan.
3   Bake cake 30 minutes. Turn onto a wire rack to cool.
4   Make passionfruit cream.
5   Split cold sponge in half; sandwich with passionfruit cream. Dust with sifted icing sugar.

PASSIONFRUIT CREAM
Beat cream and sugar in a small bowl with an electric mixer until soft peaks form; fold in passionfruit pulp.

You can use just one 300ml carton of cream for the passionfruit cream recipe.
This cake is best eaten the day it is made.

DARK GINGERBREAD *Cake*

PREP + COOK TIME *1 HOUR* MAKES *16*

125g (4 ounces) butter, softened
½ cup (110g) firmly packed dark brown sugar
2 eggs
1⅔ cups (250g) plain (all-purpose) flour
½ teaspoon bicarbonate of soda (baking soda)
2 teaspoons ground ginger
1 cup (360g) treacle
2 tablespoons milk
¼ cup (55g) finely chopped glacé ginger
⅓ cup (55g) finely chopped raisins

LEMON GLACÉ ICING
1 cup (160g) icing (confectioners') sugar
10g (½ ounce) butter, softened
1 tablespoon lemon juice
1 tablespoon boiling water, approximately

1 Preheat oven to 180°C/350°F. Grease 20cm x 30cm (8-inch x 12-inch) rectangular cake pan; line base and sides with baking paper, extending the paper 5cm (2 inches) above sides.

2 Beat butter and sugar in a small bowl with an electric mixer until light and fluffy. Beat in eggs, one at a time. Transfer mixture to a large bowl; stir in sifted flour, soda and ground ginger, treacle, milk, glacé ginger and raisins. Spread mixture into pan.

3 Bake cake about 45 minutes. Stand in pan 5 minutes; turn, top-side up, onto a wire rack to cool.

4 Meanwhile, make lemon glacé icing.

5 Spread cold cake with icing. Stand until icing is set before cutting.

LEMON GLACÉ ICING
Sift icing sugar into a medium bowl. Stir in butter, juice and enough of the water until icing is smooth and spreadable.

Iced cake will keep in an airtight container for up to three days. Uniced cake can be frozen for up to three months.

SERVING SUGGESTION
Serve warm as a dessert with cream or custard.

SEMOLINA AND YOGURT
Lemon-syrup Cake

PREP + COOK TIME *1 HOUR 10 MINUTES* SERVES *8*

250g (8 ounces) butter, softened
1 tablespoon finely grated lemon rind
1 cup (220g) caster (superfine) sugar
3 eggs, separated
1 cup (150g) self-raising flour
1 cup (160g) semolina
1 cup (280g) yogurt

LEMON SYRUP
1 cup (220g) caster (superfine) sugar
⅓ cup (80ml) lemon juice

1 Preheat oven to 180°C/350°F. Butter a 20cm (8-inch) baba pan or a deep 20cm (8-inch) round cake pan well; sprinkle with a little flour, shake out excess.

2 Beat the butter, rind and sugar in a small bowl with an electric mixer until light and fluffy. Beat in egg yolks. Transfer mixture to a large bowl; stir in sifted flour, semolina and yogurt.

3 Beat egg whites in a small bowl with an electric mixer until soft peaks form; fold egg whites into cake mixture, in two batches. Spread mixture into pan.

4 Bake cake about 50 minutes.

5 Meanwhile, make lemon syrup.

6 Stand cake in pan 5 minutes; turn onto a wire rack set over an oven tray. Pierce cake all over with a skewer; pour hot lemon syrup over hot cake.

LEMON SYRUP
Stir ingredients in a small saucepan over heat, without boiling, until sugar dissolves. Bring to the boil, without stirring; remove from heat.

This cake with keep in an airtight container for up to three days.

SERVING SUGGESTION
Serve warm with whipped cream or ice-cream.

LIME AND POPPY SEED
Syrup Cake

PREP + COOK TIME 1 HOUR 20 MINUTES SERVES 16

¼ cup (40g) poppy seeds
½ cup (125ml) milk
250g (8 ounces) butter, softened
1 tablespoon finely grated lime rind
1¼ cups (275g) caster (superfine) sugar
4 eggs
2¼ cups (335g) self-raising flour
¾ cup (110g) plain (all-purpose) flour
1 cup (240g) sour cream

LIME SYRUP

½ cup (125ml) lime juice
1 cup (250ml) water
1 cup (220g) caster (superfine) sugar

1 Preheat oven to 180°C/350°F. Grease a deep 22cm (9-inch) square cake pan.
2 Combine poppy seeds and milk in a small jug; soak 10 minutes.
3 Beat butter, rind and sugar in a small bowl with an electric mixer until light and fluffy. Beat in eggs, one at a time, beating until combined between additions. Transfer mixture to a large bowl. Stir in sifted flours, sour cream and poppy seed mixture, in two batches. Spread mixture into pan.
4 Bake cake about 1 hour.
5 Meanwhile, make lime syrup.
6 Stand cake 5 minutes, turn onto a wire rack over an oven tray. Pour hot lime syrup over hot cake.

LIME SYRUP
Stir ingredients in a small saucepan over heat, without boiling, until sugar dissolves. Simmer, uncovered, without stirring, 5 minutes.

Before you grate the lime, make sure it is at room temperature and roll it, pressing down hard with your hand, on the kitchen bench. This will help extract as much juice as possible from the fruit. You can substitute the same quantities of grated rind and juice with other citrus fruit such as lemon, mandarin, orange, blood orange etc.
This cake will keep in an airtight container for up to three days.

PEANUT BUTTER
Bundt Cake

PEANUT BUTTER
Bundt Cake

PREP + COOK TIME *1 HOUR 45 MINUTES (+ COOLING & STANDING)*
SERVES *12*

185g (6 ounces) butter, softened
1½ cups (330g) caster (superfine) sugar
2 teaspoons vanilla extract
½ cup (140g) smooth peanut butter
3 eggs
1½ cups (225g) plain (all-purpose) flour
¾ cup (110g) self-raising flour
¼ teaspoon bicarbonate of soda (baking soda)
⅔ cup (160ml) buttermilk

CHOCOLATE GLAZE
125g (4 ounces) dark eating (semi-sweet)
   chocolate, chopped coarsely
⅓ cup (80ml) thickened (heavy) cream

1 Preheat oven to 170°C/340°F. Grease a deep 22cm (9-inch) bundt pan well.
2 Beat butter, sugar, extract and peanut butter in a large bowl with an electric mixer until light and fluffy. Beat in eggs, one at a time. Sift flours and soda over butter mixture; stir to combine. Stir in buttermilk. Spread mixture into pan; smooth surface.
3 Bake cake about 1 hour. Stand in pan 5 minutes; turn onto a wire rack to cool completely.
4 Meanwhile, make chocolate glaze.
5 Pour glaze over cooled cake; stand 15 minutes before serving.

CHOCOLATE GLAZE
Stir ingredients in a small saucepan over low heat until smooth. Stand about 30 minutes or until thick.

This cake will keep in an airtight container for up to three days. Serve at room temperature.

PECAN AND DATE
Ripple Cake

PREP + COOK TIME *1 HOUR 15 MINUTES* **SERVES** *12*

125g (4 ounces) butter, softened
1 teaspoon vanilla extract
1 cup (220g) caster (superfine) sugar
2 eggs
1 cup (150g) plain (all-purpose) flour
1 cup (150g) self-raising flour
1¼ cups (300g) sour cream
½ cup (80g) coarsely chopped dried dates

PECAN TOPPING
½ cup (60g) coarsely chopped pecans
2 tablespoons demerara sugar
1 teaspoon ground cinnamon

1 Preheat oven to 180°C/350°F. Grease a deep 20cm (8-inch) round cake pan; line base with baking paper.
2 Make pecan topping.
3 Beat butter, extract and sugar in a small bowl with an electric mixer until light and fluffy. Beat in eggs, one at a time. Transfer mixture to a large bowl; stir in sifted flours, sour cream, then dates.
4 Spread half the cake mixture into pan; sprinkle with half the pecan topping. Spread with remaining cake mixture; sprinkle with remaining topping, press down lightly.
5 Bake cake about 1 hour. Stand in pan 5 minutes; turn, top-side up, onto a wire rack to cool.

PECAN TOPPING
Combine ingredients in a small bowl.

This cake will keep in an airtight container for up to three days.

(PHOTOGRAPH PAGE 124)

PECAN AND DATE
Ripple Cake
(RECIPE PAGE 123)

JAM ROLL

(RECIPE PAGE 126)

JAM ROLL

PREP + COOK TIME *30 MINUTES* SERVES *10*

3 eggs, separated
½ cup (110g) caster (superfine) sugar
2 tablespoons hot milk
¾ cup (110g) self-raising flour
¼ cup (55g) caster (superfine) sugar, extra
½ cup (160g) jam, warmed

1 Preheat oven to 200°C/400°F. Grease a 23cm x 32cm
(9-inch x 13-inch) swiss roll pan; line base and long
sides with baking paper, extending the paper 5cm
(2 inches) over sides.
2 Beat egg whites in a small bowl with an electric
mixer until soft peaks form; gradually add sugar,
beating until sugar dissolves. With motor operating,
add egg yolks, one at a time, beating until mixture
is pale and thick; this will take about 10 minutes.
3 Working quickly, pour hot milk down side of bowl;
add triple-sifted flour and fold milk and flour
through egg mixture. Spread mixture into pan.
4 Bake sponge about 8 minutes.
5 Meanwhile, place a piece of baking paper cut the
same size as the swiss roll pan on bench; sprinkle
evenly with extra sugar.
6 Turn cake immediately onto the sugared paper;
peel away lining paper. Use a serrated knife to trim
edges from all sides of cake. Using paper as a guide,
gently roll warm cake loosely from one of the
short sides. Unroll; cool. Spread evenly with jam.
Reroll cake from same short side.

Gently fold the milk and flour into the egg mixture,
taking care to keep as much air in the mixture as
possible. Heavy mixing will reduce the amount of
air incorporated in the mixture and will cause the
sponge to be flat and heavy.
Sponge roll is best eaten the day it is made.

(PHOTOGRAPH PAGE 125)

LAMINGTONS

PREP + COOK TIME *1 HOUR* MAKES *20*

6 eggs
⅔ cup (150g) caster (superfine) sugar
⅓ cup (50g) cornflour (cornstarch)
½ cup (75g) plain (all-purpose) flour
⅓ cup (50g) self-raising flour
3 cups (225g) shredded coconut
CHOCOLATE ICING
4 cups (640g) icing (confectioners') sugar
½ cup (50g) cocoa powder
15g (½ ounce) butter, melted
1 cup (250ml) milk

1 Preheat oven to 180°C/350°F. Grease a 20cm x 30cm
(8-inch x 12-inch) rectangular pan; line base and
sides with baking paper, extending the paper 5cm
(2 inches) over sides.
2 Beat eggs in a large bowl with an electric mixer
about 10 minutes or until thick and creamy;
gradually add sugar, beating until sugar dissolves.
Fold in triple-sifted flours. Spread mixture into pan.
3 Bake cake about 35 minutes. Turn cake immediately
onto a baking-paper-covered wire rack to cool.
4 Meanwhile, make chocolate icing.
5 Use serrated knife to trim edges from all sides of
cake. Cut cake into 20 squares; dip each square
in icing, drain off excess. Toss squares in coconut.
Place lamingtons onto a wire rack to set.

CHOCOLATE ICING
Sift icing sugar and cocoa into a medium heatproof
bowl; stir in butter and milk. Set bowl over a medium
saucepan of simmering water; stir until icing is of a
coating consistency.

Lamingtons will keep in an airtight container for
up to three days.

PLUM AND BLUEBERRY
Crumble Cake

PREP + COOK TIME *2 HOURS* SERVES *12*

200g (6½ ounces) butter, softened
¾ cup (165g) caster (superfine) sugar
2 eggs
1 cup (150g) self-raising flour
1 cup (150g) plain (all-purpose) flour
¾ cup (180ml) milk
1kg (2 pounds) canned whole plums
   in natural juice, drained
60g (2 ounces) fresh blueberries
2 teaspoons icing (confectioners') sugar

SPICED CRUMBLE TOPPING
½ cup (75g) plain (all-purpose) flour
50g (1½ ounces) cold butter, chopped coarsely
¾ cup (60g) shredded coconut
¼ cup (55g) firmly packed light brown sugar
1 teaspoon mixed spice

1. Preheat oven to 180°C/350°F. Grease a deep 22cm (9-inch) springform pan; line base and side with baking paper.
2. Make spiced crumble topping.
3. Beat butter and sugar in a medium bowl with an electric mixer until light and fluffy. Beat in eggs, one at a time. Transfer mixture to a large bowl; fold in sifted flours and milk, in two batches. Spread mixture into pan.
4. Halve plums; discard seeds. Place with plums and blueberries on cake mixture. Sprinkle crumble topping over fruit.
5. Bake cake about 1½ hours (cover cake with foil if browning too quickly). Stand in pan 10 minutes; remove from pan, transfer to a wire rack to cool. Serve cake warm or at room temperature.

SPICED CRUMBLE TOPPING
Blend or process ingredients until combined.

This cake will keep in an airtight container, refrigerated, for up to three days. Reheat slices in the microwave to serve warm.

SERVING SUGGESTION
Serve with thick (double) cream.

LITTLE CHOCOLATE
and Coconut Sponges

PREP + COOK TIME *50 MINUTES* **MAKES** *18*

4 eggs
¾ cup (165g) caster (superfine) sugar
⅔ cup (100g) self-raising flour
⅓ cup (35g) cocoa powder
90g (3 ounces) butter, melted
1 tablespoon hot water
⅔ cup (160ml) thickened (heavy) cream
2 tablespoons caster (superfine) sugar, extra
⅓ cup (15g) flaked coconut

CHOCOLATE GANACHE
200g (6½ ounces) dark eating (semi-sweet)
   chocolate, chopped coarsely
⅔ cup (160ml) thickened (heavy) cream

1 Preheat oven to 180°C/350°F. Grease two 9-hole (½-cup/125ml) friand pans.
2 Beat eggs in a small bowl with an electric mixer until thick and creamy. Beat in sugar, a tablespoon at a time, until dissolved. Transfer mixture to a large bowl; fold in sifted flour and cocoa, then butter and the hot water. Spoon mixture into pan holes.
3 Bake sponges about 12 minutes. Turn immediately onto baking-paper-covered wire racks to cool.
4 Meanwhile, make chocolate ganache.
5 Beat cream and extra sugar in a small bowl with an electric mixer until soft peaks form.
6 Split cold sponges in half. Spread bases with cream; replace tops. Spread ganache on cakes; top with coconut.

CHOCOLATE GANACHE
Stir ingredients in a small saucepan over low heat until smooth. Remove from heat; stand until thickened.

Filled sponges are best eaten the day they are made. Unfilled sponges can be frozen for up to one month.

GRATED CHOCOLATE
Sponge Roll

PREP + COOK TIME 30 MINUTES (+ COOLING) SERVES 10

4 eggs, separated
½ cup (110g) caster (superfine) sugar
2 tablespoons hot water
60g (2 ounces) dark eating (semi-sweet) chocolate, grated coarsely
½ cup (75g) self-raising flour
2 tablespoons caster (superfine) sugar, extra

VANILLA CREAM
¾ cup (180ml) thickened (heavy) cream
2 teaspoons icing (confectioners') sugar
1 teaspoon vanilla extract

1 Preheat oven to 180°C/350°F. Grease a 23cm x 32cm (9-inch x 13-inch) swiss roll pan; line base and long sides with baking paper, extending the paper 5cm (2 inches) over sides.
2 Beat egg yolks and sugar in a small bowl with an electric mixer about 5 minutes or until thick and creamy. Transfer mixture to a large bowl; fold in the hot water and chocolate, then fold in sifted flour.
3 Beat egg whites in a small bowl with an electric mixer until soft peaks form; fold into chocolate mixture. Spread mixture into pan.
4 Bake sponge about 12 minutes.

5 Meanwhile, place a piece of baking paper cut the same size as pan on bench; sprinkle with extra sugar.
6 Turn hot sponge onto the sugared paper; peel away lining paper. Using paper as a guide, loosely roll sponge from long side. Stand 2 minutes; unroll. Cool; trim all sides of sponge.
7 Make vanilla cream.
8 Spread sponge with vanilla cream. Using paper as a guide, roll sponge from long side.

VANILLA CREAM
Beat ingredients in a small bowl with an electric mixer until soft peaks form.

Filled sponge roll is best eaten the day it is made; keep in an airtight container, refrigerated, until ready to serve.

SERVING SUGGESTION
Serve sponge roll topped with grated dark eating chocolate or small chocolate curls.

MARBLE CAKE

PREP + COOK TIME *1 HOUR 40 MINUTES* **SERVES** *12*

250g (8 ounces) butter, softened
1 teaspoon vanilla extract
1¼ cups (275g) caster (superfine) sugar
3 eggs
2¼ cups (335g) self-raising flour
¾ cup (180ml) milk
pink food colouring
2 tablespoons cocoa powder
2 tablespoons milk, extra

BUTTER FROSTING
125g (4 ounces) butter, softened
2 cups (320g) icing (confectioners') sugar
2 tablespoons milk

1 Preheat oven to 180°C/350°F. Grease a deep 22cm (9-inch) round cake pan; line base with baking paper.
2 Beat butter, extract and sugar in a medium bowl with an electric mixer until light and fluffy. Beat in eggs, one at a time. Stir in sifted flour and milk, in two batches.
3 Divide mixture into three bowls; tint one mixture pink. Blend sifted cocoa with extra milk in a cup; stir into second mixture. Leave remaining mixture plain. Drop alternate spoonfuls of mixtures into pan. Pull a skewer backwards and forwards through cake mixture to create a marble effect.
4 Bake cake about 1 hour. Stand in pan 5 minutes; turn, top-side up, onto a wire rack to cool.
5 Meanwhile, make butter frosting.
6 Spread frosting all over cold cake.

BUTTER FROSTING
Beat butter in a small bowl with an electric mixer until light and fluffy; beat in sifted icing sugar and milk, in two batches.

The traditional colours for a marble cake are chocolate brown, pink and white, but you can use any food colouring you like. Make the colours fairly strong for maximum impact, as they may fade during baking.
This cake will keep in an airtight container, at room temperature, for up to three days. Uniced cake can be frozen for up to three months.

SPICED SPONGE
with Pistachio Honey Cream

PREP + COOK TIME *40 MINUTES* SERVES *10*

4 eggs

¾ cup (165g) firmly packed dark brown sugar

1 cup (150g) wheaten cornflour (cornstarch)

1 teaspoon cream of tartar

½ teaspoon bicarbonate of soda (baking soda)

1 teaspoon mixed spice

½ teaspoon ground cardamom

2 teaspoons icing (confectioners') sugar

PISTACHIO HONEY CREAM

1 cup (250ml) thickened (heavy) cream

1 tablespoon honey

¼ cup (30g) finely chopped roasted
   unsalted pistachios

1 Preheat oven to 180°C/350°F. Grease two deep 22cm (9-inch) round cake pans.

2 Beat eggs and sugar in a small bowl with an electric mixer about 10 minutes or until sugar dissolves and mixture is thick and creamy; transfer to a large bowl.

3 Gently fold triple-sifted dry ingredients into egg mixture. Divide mixture into pans.

4 Bake sponges about 18 minutes. Turn sponges immediately, top-side up, onto baking-paper-covered wire racks to cool.

5 Meanwhile, make pistachio honey cream.

6 Sandwich sponges with pistachio honey cream; dust with sifted icing sugar.

PISTACHIO HONEY CREAM

Beat cream and honey in a small bowl with an electric mixer until soft peaks form; fold in nuts.

Beat the eggs and sugar until they have tripled in volume; the trapped air will make the sponge as light as a feather. Sifting the dry ingredients three times will add lots of air to the sponge, making it light and soft.

Filled, this sponge is best eaten the day it is made. Unfilled sponges can be frozen for up to two months.

RASPBERRY CREAM
Sponge

PREP + COOK TIME *50 MINUTES (+ COOLING)* SERVES *16*

4 eggs
¾ cup (165g) caster (superfine) sugar
⅔ cup (100g) wheaten cornflour (cornstarch)
¼ cup (30g) custard powder
1 teaspoon cream of tartar
½ teaspoon bicarbonate of soda (baking soda)
1½ cups (375ml) thickened (heavy) cream
¾ cup (240g) raspberry jam

RASPBERRY GLACÉ ICING
45g (1½ ounces) fresh raspberries
2 cups (320g) icing (confectioners') sugar
15g (½ ounce) butter, softened
2 teaspoons hot water, approximately

1 Preheat oven to 180°C/350°F. Grease a deep 22cm (9-inch) square cake pan.
2 Beat eggs and sugar in a small bowl with an electric mixer about 10 minutes or until thick and creamy and sugar has dissolved; transfer to a large bowl.
3 Sift dry ingredients twice, then sift a third time over egg mixture; fold dry ingredients into egg mixture. Spread mixture into pan.
4 Bake sponge about 25 minutes. Turn immediately onto a baking-paper-covered wire rack, then turn top-side up to cool.
5 Meanwhile, make raspberry glacé icing.
6 Beat cream in a small bowl with an electric mixer until soft peaks form.
7 Split sponge in half. Place bottom half of sponge on a serving plate or stand; spread with jam and cream. Top with remaining sponge half; spread top with icing. Serve topped with fresh rose petals, if you like.

RASPBERRY GLACÉ ICING
Push raspberries through a fine sieve into a small heatproof bowl; discard solids. Sift icing sugar into same bowl; stir in butter and enough of the water to make a thick paste. Place bowl over a small saucepan of simmering water; stir mixture until icing is spreadable.

Use a serrated or electric knife to split and cut the sponge.
Filled, this sponge is best eaten the day it is made. Unfilled sponge can be frozen for up to two months.

CHAPTER 4
PASTRIES & WHOOPIES

CHOCOLATE, PLUM AND ALMOND
Paris Brest

PREP + COOK TIME *1 HOUR 30 MINUTES (+ STANDING)* **MAKES** *20*

½ cup (125ml) water
60g (2 ounces) butter
1 tablespoon caster (superfine) sugar
⅔ cup (100g) plain (all-purpose) flour
3 eggs
90g (3 ounces) dark eating (semi-sweet)
   chocolate, chopped coarsely
1 teaspoon vegetable oil
¼ cup (20g) flaked almonds, roasted
8 drained canned plums (275g),
   chopped coarsely

VANILLA CUSTARD CREAM

2 tablespoons cornflour (cornstarch)
2 tablespoons custard powder
¼ cup (55g) caster (superfine) sugar
1¼ cups (310ml) thickened (heavy) cream
¾ cup (180ml) milk
1 teaspoon vanilla extract
15g (½ ounce) butter
1 egg yolk
¾ cup (180ml) thickened (heavy) cream, extra

1 Make vanilla custard cream.
2 Preheat oven to 220°C/425°F. Grease oven trays.
3 To make choux pastry, combine the water, butter and sugar in a medium saucepan; bring to the boil. Add flour, beat with a wooden spoon over heat until mixture comes away from base of pan. Transfer pastry to a medium bowl; beat in eggs, one at a time with an electric mixer until pastry becomes smooth and glossy but will hold its shape.
4 Spoon pastry into a piping bag fitted with a 1.5cm (¾-inch) plain tube; pipe 5cm (2-inch) rings, about 5cm (2 inches) apart on trays.
5 Bake 10 minutes. Reduce oven to 180°C/350°F; bake a futher 15 minutes. Using a serrated knife, split rings in half, remove any soft centres; return to trays, bake further 5 minutes or until pastry rings are dry. Cool on trays.
6 Place chocolate and oil in a small heatproof bowl over a small saucepan of simmering water, stirring, until melted. Spread pastry tops with chocolate, sprinkle with nuts. Stand until chocolate is set.
7 Spoon custard cream into a piping bag fitted with a 2cm (¾-inch) fluted tube. Pipe custard cream on to pastry bases; top with plums. Top with pastry tops.

VANILLA CUSTARD CREAM

Combine cornflour, custard powder and sugar in a medium saucepan. Gradually add combined cream, milk and extract; stir over low heat until mixture boils and thickens. Add butter; simmer, stirring, 3 minutes. Remove from heat; stir in egg yolk. Place custard in a medium bowl; cover surface with plastic wrap, cool. Beat extra cream in a small bowl with an electric mixer until firm peaks form. Whisk custard until smooth; fold in whipped cream.

You need half a 1kg (2-pound) can plums for this recipe. You can use fresh plums when in season. Fill pastries up to an hour before serving.

LEMON MERINGUE
Tartlets

PREP + COOK TIME *30 MINUTES (+ REFRIGERATION)* **MAKES** *24*

4 egg yolks
⅓ cup (75g) caster (superfine) sugar
2 teaspoons finely grated lemon rind
¼ cup (60ml) lemon juice
40g (1½ ounces) unsalted butter, chopped
24 x 4.5cm (1¾-inch) diameter baked
   pastry cases

MERINGUE
1 egg white
¼ cup (55g) caster (superfine) sugar

1 Combine egg yolks, sugar, rind, juice and butter in a small heatproof bowl; stir over a small saucepan of simmering water until mixture thickens slightly and coats the back of a spoon. Remove pan from heat, remove bowl from pan immediately. Cover surface of lemon curd with plastic wrap; refrigerate until cold.
2 Preheat oven to 200°C/400°F.
3 Meanwhile, make meringue.
4 Place pastry cases on oven tray; fill with curd, then top with meringue.
5 Bake tartlets about 5 minutes or until meringue is browned lightly.

MERINGUE
Beat egg white in a small bowl with an electric mixer until soft peaks form; gradually add sugar, beating until sugar dissolves.

To make your own cases, cut 7cm (2¾-inch) rounds from two sheets shortcrust pastry. Press pastry rounds into two 12-hole (1½-tablespoon/30ml) mini muffin pans; bake about 10 minutes or until browned lightly.
Serve tartlets within an hour of being made.

BAKLAVA

PREP + COOK TIME *1 HOUR 20 MINUTES (+ COOLING)* **MAKES** *30*

1½ cups (200g) unsalted shelled pistachios
2 cups (200g) walnut pieces
¼ cup (55g) caster (superfine) sugar
2 tablespoons fine semolina
1 teaspoon ground cinnamon
pinch ground cloves
375g (12 ounces) fillo pastry
310g (10 ounces) butter, melted
30 whole cloves

SYRUP

1 cup (220g) caster (superfine) sugar
1 cup (250ml) water
¼ cup (90g) honey
1 tablespoon lemon juice
1 cinnamon stick

1 Preheat oven to 200°C/400°F. Grease a 20cm x 30cm (8-inch x 12-inch) rectangular pan.
2 Process nuts, sugar, semolina, cinnamon and ground cloves until chopped finely; transfer to a medium bowl.
3 Brush 1 sheet of pastry with a little of the butter; top with 7 more sheets, brushing each well with butter. Fold pastry in half, place into pan. Sprinkle pastry with thin even layer of the nut mixture. Layer another 2 sheets of pastry, brushing each well with more butter. Fold pastry in half, place in pan; top with another layer of nut mixture. Repeat layering process until all nut mixture has been used. Repeat layering and buttering with any remaining pastry sheets; brush the final layer with butter. Score the top lightly in a diamond pattern; press one whole clove in the centre of each piece.
4 Bake baklava about 50 minutes.
5 Meanwhile, make syrup.
6 Pour syrup over hot baklava. Cool before cutting.

SYRUP

Stir ingredients in a small saucepan over heat, without boiling, until sugar dissolves; bring to the boil. Reduce heat; simmer, uncovered, about 10 minutes or until thickened slightly. Discard cinnamon; cool syrup.

Baklava will keep in an airtight container for up to one week.

ORANGE AND ALMOND
Palmiers

PREP + COOK TIME *45 MINUTES (+ REFRIGERATION)* **MAKES 32**

1 cup (150g) vienna almonds
15g (½ ounce) butter
2 tablespoons orange-flavoured liqueur
2 teaspoons finely grated orange rind
2 tablespoons demerara sugar
2 sheets butter puff pastry
1 egg, beaten lightly

1 Blend or process nuts, butter, liqueur and rind to a coarse paste.

2 Sprinkle a board with half the sugar; place one sheet of pastry on the sugar. Roll pastry gently into sugar. Spread half the nut mixture over pastry; fold two opposite sides of pastry inwards to meet in the middle. Flatten folded pastry slightly; brush with a little egg. Fold each side in half to meet in the middle; flatten slightly. Fold the two sides in half again so they touch in the middle. Repeat process with remaining sugar, pastry, nut mixture and egg. Enclose pastry rolls in plastic wrap; refrigerate 30 minutes.

3 Preheat oven to 200°C/400°F. Grease oven trays.

4 Cut pastry rolls into 1cm (½-inch) slices; place slices about 2.5cm (1 inch) apart on trays.

5 Bake palmiers about 12 minutes. Transfer to wire racks to cool.

Palmiers are best eaten on the day they are made.

CHOCOLATE ÉCLAIRS

PREP + COOK TIME *1 HOUR (+ REFRIGERATION & COOLING)* MAKES *16*

15g (½ ounce) butter
¼ cup (60ml) water
¼ cup (35g) plain (all-purpose) flour
1 egg

CUSTARD CREAM
1 vanilla bean
1 cup (250ml) milk
3 egg yolks
⅓ cup (75g) caster (superfine) sugar
2 tablespoons 100% corn (maize) cornflour
   (cornstarch)
⅓ cup (80ml) thickened (heavy) cream

CHOCOLATE GLAZE
30g (1 ounce) dark eating (semi-sweet)
   chocolate, chopped coarsely
30g (1 ounce) milk eating chocolate,
   chopped coarsely
15g (½ ounce) butter

1 Make custard cream.
2 Preheat oven to 220°C/425°F. Grease two oven trays.
3 Combine butter and the water in a small saucepan; bring to the boil. Add flour, beat with wooden spoon over heat until mixture comes away from side of pan and forms a smooth ball. Transfer mixture to a small bowl; beat in egg with an electric mixer until mixture becomes glossy.
4 Spoon pastry mixture into a piping bag fitted with a 1cm (½-inch) plain tube. Pipe 5cm (2-inch) lengths, about 5cm (2 inches) apart on trays.

5 Bake 7 minutes. Reduce oven to 180°C/350°F; bake further 10 minutes. Using a serrated knife, cut éclairs in half, remove any soft centres; return to trays, bake 5 minutes or until dry to touch. Cool on trays.
6 Make chocolate glaze.
7 Spoon custard cream into a piping bag fitted with a 5mm (¼-inch) fluted tube. Pipe custard cream into 16 pastry bases, top with pastry tops. Spread with chocolate glaze.

CUSTARD CREAM
Split vanilla bean lengthways, scrape seeds into milk in a small saucepan (discard bean); bring to the boil. Beat egg yolks, sugar and cornflour in a small bowl with an electric mixer until thick. With motor operating, gradually beat in hot milk mixture. Return custard to pan; stir over heat until mixture boils and thickens. Cover surface with plastic wrap; refrigerate 1 hour. Beat cream in a small bowl with an electric mixer until soft peaks form. Just before serving, fold cream into custard, in two batches.

CHOCOLATE GLAZE
Stir ingredients in a small heatproof bowl over a small saucepan of simmering water until smooth. Use while warm.

Éclairs and custard cream can be made and stored separately, two days ahead; fold cream into custard just before using. Assemble and serve éclairs as close to serving time as possible – about an hour.

LEMON CRÈME BRÛLÉE
Tarts

PREP + COOK TIME *1 HOUR 10 MINUTES (+ REFRIGERATION & COOLING)* MAKES *24*

1¼ cups (310ml) pouring cream (see notes)
⅓ cup (80ml) milk
4 x 5cm (2-inch) strips lemon rind
4 egg yolks
¼ cup (55g) caster (superfine) sugar

PASTRY

1¾ cups (260g) plain (all-purpose) flour
¼ cup (40g) icing (confectioners') sugar
2 teaspoons finely grated lemon rind
185g (6 ounces) cold butter, chopped coarsely
1 egg yolk
2 teaspoons iced water, approximately

TOFFEE

1 cup (220g) caster (superfine) sugar
½ cup (125ml) water

1 Make pastry.
2 Grease two 12-hole (1½-tablespoon/30ml) shallow round-based patty pans.
3 Divide pastry in half. Roll one half between sheets of baking paper until 3mm (⅛-inch) thick. Cut out 12 x 6cm (2¼-inch) fluted rounds; press rounds into pan holes. Prick bases of cases well with a fork. Repeat with remaining pastry. Refrigerate 30 minutes.
4 Preheat oven to 160°C/325°F.
5 Combine cream, milk and rind in a small saucepan; bring to the boil. Beat egg yolks and sugar in a small bowl with an electric mixer until thick and creamy. Gradually beat hot cream mixture into egg mixture; allow bubbles to subside. Strain custard into a medium jug, pour into pastry cases.
6 Bake tarts about 25 minutes. Cool. Refrigerate 2 hours.
7 Make toffee.
8 Remove tarts from pan; place on an oven tray. Sprinkle custard with toffee; using a blowtorch, heat until toffee caramelises.

PASTRY

Process flour, sugar, rind and butter until crumbly. With motor operating, add egg yolk and enough of the water to make ingredients come together. Knead dough on a floured surface until smooth. Wrap in plastic wrap; refrigerate 30 minutes.

TOFFEE

Stir sugar and the water in a medium saucepan over heat, without boiling, until sugar dissolves. Bring to the boil; boil, uncovered, without stirring, until golden brown. Pour toffee on a greased oven tray to set. Break toffee into large pieces; process until chopped finely.

You can use just one 300ml carton of cream for this recipe.
Blowtorches are available from kitchenware and hardware stores.
These tarts are best eaten on the day they are made. If the weather is humid, caramelise the toffee about 30 minutes before serving.

SUGARY CINNAMON
Twists

PREP + COOK TIME *25 MINUTES* MAKES *25*

1 sheet puff pastry
20g (¾ ounce) butter, melted
2 tablespoons raw sugar
½ teaspoon ground cinnamon

1 Preheat oven to 200°C/400°F. Grease oven trays.
2 Brush pastry with butter; sprinkle with combined sugar and cinnamon. Cut pastry in half. Turn one half over, sugar-side down; place the other half, sugar-side up, on top. Press lightly to join layers. Cut pastry into 1cm (½-inch) wide strips; twist each strip, pinching ends to secure. Place on trays.
3 Bake about 10 minutes or until browned lightly and crisp; transfer to a wire rack to cool.

Twists are at their best eaten on the day they are made, but they will keep, in an airtight container, for up to two days.

FIG GALETTES

PREP + COOK TIME *30 MINUTES* MAKES *4*

1 sheet puff pastry
⅓ cup (40g) ground almonds
4 large fresh figs (320g), sliced thinly
30g (1 ounce) butter, melted
2 tablespoons pure maple syrup
2 teaspoons icing (confectioners') sugar

1 Preheat oven to 180°C/350°F. Line an oven tray with baking paper.
2 Cut 4 x 12cm (4¾-inch) rounds from pastry; sprinkle with ground almonds. Top with figs; brush with combined butter and syrup. Turn edges of pastry up.
3 Bake galettes about 20 minutes or until pastry is puffed and golden. Serve warm, dusted with sifted icing sugar.

Galettes are best served warm.

SERVING SUGGESTION
Serve with thick (double) cream or ice-cream.

SUGARY CINNAMON
Twists

FIG GALETTES

CHOCOLATE MOUSSE
Puffs

PREP + COOK TIME *1 HOUR (+ REFRIGERATION)* MAKES *32*

1 cup (250ml) water
80g (2½ ounces) butter, chopped coarsely
1 cup (150g) plain (all-purpose) flour
2 tablespoons cocoa powder
4 eggs
2 teaspoons drinking chocolate

CHOCOLATE MOUSSE FILLING
1⅔ cups (250g) white chocolate Melts
2⅓ cups (580ml) thickened (heavy) cream
   (see notes)
125g (4 ounces) cream cheese, softened
⅔ cup (150g) caster (superfine) sugar
2 egg yolks

1 Make chocolate mousse filling.
2 Preheat oven to 220°C/425°F. Grease oven trays.
3 Bring the water and butter to the boil in a small saucepan. Add sifted flour and cocoa, beat with a wooden spoon over heat until mixture comes away from side of pan and forms a smooth ball.
4 Transfer mixture to a small bowl; beat in eggs, one at a time, with an electric mixer until mixture becomes glossy. Drop level tablespoons of mixture, 4cm (1½ inches) apart, onto trays.
5 Bake about 15 minutes or until pastry is puffed. Using a skewer, make a small hole in base of each puff; cool on wire racks.

6 Reduce oven to 200°C/400°F.
7 Split puffs in half, use a teaspoon to scoop out any uncooked mixture; return halves, cut-side up, to oven trays. Bake about 10 minutes or until puffs are crisp; cool on wire racks.
8 Just before serving, spoon mousse filling into bottom half of puffs, replace tops. Serve puffs dusted with sifted drinking chocolate.

CHOCOLATE MOUSSE FILLING
Stir chocolate in a small heatproof bowl over a small saucepan of simmering water until melted. Beat cream in a medium bowl with an electric mixer until soft peaks form. Beat cream cheese, sugar and egg yolks in a large bowl with electric mixer until smooth. Just before melted chocolate sets, beat into cheese mixture then fold in cream, in two batches. Cover; refrigerate until cold.

You can use one 600ml (or two 300ml) carton of cream for this recipe.
Unfilled puffs and chocolate mousse filling can be made a day ahead; assemble no more than an hour before serving.

LEMON CURD AND
Poppy Seed Pastries

PREP + COOK TIME *45 MINUTES* (+ REFRIGERATION) MAKES *24*

1¾ cups (260g) plain (all-purpose) flour
⅓ cup (55g) icing (confectioners') sugar
185g (6 ounces) cold unsalted butter, chopped coarsely
2 tablespoons poppy seeds
1 egg yolk
2 teaspoons iced water, approximately
⅓ cup (80ml) thick (double) cream

LEMON CURD

2 egg yolks
¼ cup (55g) caster (superfine) sugar
2 teaspoons finely grated lemon rind
2 tablespoons lemon juice
100g (3 ounces) cold unsalted butter, chopped coarsely

1 Make lemon curd.
2 Process flour, icing sugar, butter and poppy seeds until crumbly. With motor operating, add egg yolk and enough of the water to make ingredients come together. Turn dough onto a floured surface, knead gently until smooth. Roll out half the pastry between sheets of baking paper until 3mm (⅛-inch) thick. Repeat with remaining pastry. Place on trays; refrigerate 30 minutes.
3 Grease two 12-hole (1-tablespoon/20ml) mini muffin pans. Cut 24 x 5.5cm (2¼-inch) rounds from pastry; press rounds into pan holes. Prick bases of pastry cases well with a fork. Refrigerate 30 minutes.
4 Preheat oven to 220°C/425°F.
5 Bake pastry cases about 12 minutes. Stand cases in pan 10 minutes; transfer to a wire rack to cool.
6 Spoon lemon curd into cases; top with cream.

LEMON CURD

Whisk egg yolks and sugar in a small heatproof bowl until pale and thickened slightly. Whisk in rind and juice; stir over a small saucepan of simmering water about 12 minutes or until mixture coats the back of a spoon. Remove from heat; gradually whisk in butter until combined between additions. Cover surface of curd with plastic wrap; refrigerate overnight.

Assemble pastries no more than an hour before serving; refrigerate until required.

RASPBERRY ALMOND
Crumble Tart

RASPBERRY ALMOND
Crumble Tart

PREP + COOK TIME *1 HOUR (+ REFRIGERATION & COOLING)* **SERVES** *8*

1½ cups (225g) frozen raspberries
1 teaspoon icing (confectioners') sugar

ALMOND CRUMBLE PASTRY
150g (4½ ounces) butter, softened
1 teaspoon vanilla extract
⅔ cup (150g) caster (superfine) sugar
1 egg
½ cup (60g) ground almonds
1½ cups (225g) plain (all-purpose) flour

1 Make almond crumble pastry.
2 Roll two-thirds of the pastry between sheets of baking paper until large enough to a line 11cm x 35cm (4½-inch x 14-inch) rectangular loose-based flan tin. Lift pastry into tin, press into base and sides; trim edges. Prick pastry base with a fork; refrigerate 30 minutes. Reserve remaining pastry.
3 Preheat oven to 200°C/400°F.
4 Place flan tin on an oven tray; bake about 10 minutes or until browned lightly. Sprinkle raspberries over base, sprinkle with remaining crumbled pastry. Bake a further 20 minutes or until browned; cool in pan. Dust with a little extra icing sugar before serving.

ALMOND CRUMBLE PASTRY
Beat butter in a small bowl with an electric mixer until smooth. Add extract, sugar and egg; beat until combined. Stir in ground almonds and half the flour. Work in remaining flour using your hand. Knead pastry on a floured surface until smooth. Enclose with plastic wrap; refrigerate 30 minutes.

This recipe is best made on day of serving as the raspberries will soften the pastry.

SERVING SUGGESTION
Serve with thick (double) cream, ice-cream or custard.

SPICY BANANA
Whoopie Pies

PREP + COOK TIME *45 MINUTES* **MAKES** *20*

125g (4 ounces) butter, softened
½ cup (110g) firmly packed light brown sugar
1 egg
⅓ cup mashed banana
⅔ cup (160ml) buttermilk
1¼ cups (185g) plain (all-purpose) flour
¼ cup (35g) self-raising flour
1 teaspoon bicarbonate of soda (baking soda)
1 teaspoon mixed spice
2 teaspoons icing (confectioners') sugar

LEMON CREAM CHEESE FILLING
100g (3 ounces) cream cheese, softened
1 teaspoon finely grated lemon rind
1 cup (160g) icing (confectioners') sugar

1 Preheat oven to 200°C/400°F. Grease oven trays; line with baking paper.
2 Beat butter, sugar and egg in a medium bowl with an electric mixer until light and fluffy. Stir in banana, buttermilk and sifted flours, soda and spice.
3 Drop level tablespoons of mixture about 5cm (2 inches) apart onto trays; tap trays lightly on the bench to spread slightly.
4 Bake pies about 10 minutes. Cool on trays.
5 Meanwhile, make lemon cream cheese filling.
6 Sandwich pies with filling; dust with icing sugar.

LEMON CREAM CHEESE FILLING
Beat ingredients in a small bowl with an electric mixer until smooth.

You need one small overripe banana (130g) for the amount of mashed banana used in this recipe. Whoopie pies are best eaten the day they are made.

(PHOTOGRAPH PAGE 162)

SPICY BANANA
Whoopie Pies
(RECIPE PAGE 161)

GINGER AND LIME
Whoopie Pies
(RECIPE PAGE 164)

GINGER AND LIME
Whoopie Pies

PREP + COOK TIME *45 MINUTES* **MAKES** *20*

125g (4 ounces) butter, softened
⅔ cup (150g) firmly packed light brown sugar
1 egg
⅔ cup (160ml) buttermilk
½ cup (40g) desiccated coconut
1¼ cups (185g) plain (all-purpose) flour
¼ cup (35g) self-raising flour
1 teaspoon bicarbonate of soda (baking soda)
1 tablespoon ground ginger
¼ teaspoon ground cloves

LIME BUTTERCREAM
100g (3 ounces) butter, softened
1 teaspoon finely grated lime rind
1 cup (160g) icing (confectioners') sugar

1 Preheat oven to 200°C/400°F. Grease oven trays; line with baking paper.
2 Beat butter, sugar and egg in a medium bowl with an electric mixer until light and fluffy. Stir in buttermilk, coconut and sifted flours, soda and spices.
3 Drop level tablespoons of mixture about 5cm (2 inches) apart onto trays; tap trays lightly on the bench to spread slightly.
4 Bake pies about 10 minutes. Cool on trays.
5 Meanwhile, make lime buttercream.
6 Sandwich pies with buttercream.

LIME BUTTERCREAM
Beat butter in a small bowl with an electric mixer until as white as possible. Beat in rind and sifted icing sugar until smooth.

Whoopie pies are best eaten the day they are made.

(PHOTOGRAPH PAGE 163)

CARAMEL APPLE
Whoopie Pies

PREP + COOK TIME *45 MINUTES* **MAKES** *20*

125g (4 ounces) butter, softened
⅓ cup (75g) firmly packed light brown sugar
1 egg
1 tablespoon treacle
⅔ cup (160ml) buttermilk
1 small green-skinned apple (130g)
1¼ cups (185g) plain (all-purpose) flour
¼ cup (35g) self-raising flour
1 teaspoon bicarbonate of soda (baking soda)
½ cup (125ml) thickened (heavy) cream
⅓ cup (110g) caramel top 'n' fill

1 Preheat oven to 200°C/400°F. Grease oven trays; line with baking paper.
2 Beat butter, sugar and egg in a medium bowl with an electric mixer until light and fluffy. Stir in buttermilk, coarsely grated apple and sifted flours and soda.
3 Drop level tablespoons of mixture about 5cm (2 inches) apart onto trays; tap trays lightly on the bench to spread slightly.
4 Bake pies about 10 minutes. Cool on trays.
5 Meanwhile, beat cream in a small bowl with an electric mixer until firm peaks form.
6 Sandwich pies with cream and caramel.

Whoopie pies are best eaten the day they are made.

CARAMEL APPLE
Whoopie Pies

WHITE CHOCOLATE AND PASSIONFRUIT
Whoopie Pies

PREP + COOK TIME *50 MINUTES* MAKES *20*

125g (4 ounces) unsalted butter, softened
½ cup (110g) caster (superfine) sugar
1 egg
1 ¼ cups (185g) plain (all-purpose) flour
¼ cup (35g) self-raising flour
1 teaspoon bicarbonate of soda (baking soda)
½ cup (125ml) buttermilk
100g (3 ounces) white eating chocolate, grated coarsely
2 tablespoons passionfruit pulp
2 tablespoons icing (confectioners') sugar

PASSIONFRUIT MARSHMALLOW FILLING
2 egg whites
⅔ cup (150g) caster (superfine) sugar
1 tablespoon glucose syrup
2 tablespoons passionfruit juice
yellow food colouring

1 Preheat oven to 200°C/400°F. Grease oven trays; line with baking paper.
2 Beat butter, caster sugar and egg in a small bowl with an electric mixer until light and fluffy. Beat in sifted dry ingredients and buttermilk, on low speed, until smooth. Stir in chocolate and passionfruit.
3 Drop level tablespoons of mixture about 5cm (2 inches) apart onto trays.
4 Bake pies about 10 minutes. Cool on trays.
5 Meanwhile, make passionfruit marshmallow filling.
6 Spoon marshmallow filling into a piping bag fitted with a 2cm (¾-inch) fluted tube. Pipe filling on flat side of half the cooled pies; sandwich with remaining pies. Serve dusted with sifted icing sugar.

PASSIONFRUIT MARSHMALLOW FILLING
Place ingredients in a medium heatproof bowl set over a medium saucepan of simmering water (do not allow water to touch base of bowl). Whisk vigorously about 10 minutes or until thick and creamy. Remove from heat; transfer mixture to a large heatproof bowl. Beat with an electric mixer, on high speed, about 5 minutes or until mixture is thick and holds its shape.

Whoopie pies are best eaten the day they are made.

CAPPUCCINO
Whoopie Pies

PREP + COOK TIME *50 MINUTES* MAKES *20*

2 tablespoons instant coffee granules

1 tablespoon boiling water

125g (4 ounces) unsalted butter, softened

½ cup (110g) caster (superfine) sugar

1 egg

1¼ cups (185g) plain (all-purpose) flour

¼ cup (35g) self-raising flour

1 tablespoon cocoa powder

1 teaspoon bicarbonate of soda (baking soda)

⅔ cup (160ml) buttermilk

1 tablespoon dark cocoa powder

VANILLA CREAM CHEESE FILLING

250g (8 ounces) cream cheese, softened

¼ cup (40g) icing (confectioners') sugar

2 teaspoons vanilla bean paste

⅔ cup (160ml) thickened (heavy) cream

1 Preheat oven to 200°C/400°F. Grease oven trays; line with baking paper.

2 Dissolve coffee granules in the water in a small jug.

3 Beat butter, sugar and egg in a small bowl with an electric mixer until light and fluffy. Beat in sifted flours, cocoa and soda, buttermilk and coffee mixture, on low speed, until mixture is smooth.

4 Drop level tablespoons of mixture about 5cm (2 inches) apart onto trays.

5 Bake pies about 10 minutes. Cool on trays.

6 Meanwhile, make vanilla cream cheese filling.

7 Spoon filling into a piping bag fitted with a 2cm (¾-inch) fluted tube. Pipe filling on flat side of half the cooled pies; sandwich with remaining pies. Serve dusted with dark cocoa powder.

VANILLA CREAM CHEESE FILLING
Beat cream cheese, sugar and vanilla bean paste in a small bowl with an electric mixer until smooth. Beat in cream.

Whoopie pies are best eaten the day they are made.

LAMINGTON
Whoopie Pies

PREP + COOK TIME *55 MINUTES* MAKES *20*

125g (4 ounces) unsalted butter, softened
½ cup (110g) firmly packed light brown sugar
1 egg
¾ cup (110g) plain (all-purpose) flour
⅓ cup (35g) cocoa powder
¼ cup (35g) self-raising flour
1 teaspoon bicarbonate of soda (baking soda)
⅔ cup (160ml) buttermilk
1¼ cups (310ml) thickened (heavy) cream
   (see note)
⅓ cup (110g) raspberry jam
3 tablespoons shredded coconut

CHOCOLATE GANACHE
¼ cup (60ml) pouring cream
180g (5½ ounces) dark eating (semi-sweet)
   chocolate, chopped finely

1 Preheat oven to 200°C/400°F. Grease oven trays;
   line with baking paper.
2 Beat butter, sugar and egg in a small bowl with an
   electric mixer until light and fluffy. Beat in sifted
   dry ingredients and buttermilk, on low speed,
   until mixture is smooth.
3 Drop level tablespoons of mixture about 5cm
   (2 inches) apart onto trays.
4 Bake about 10 minutes. Cool on trays.
5 Meanwhile, make chocolate ganache.
6 Beat cream in a small bowl with an electric mixer
   until firm peaks form. Spoon whipped cream into
   a piping bag fitted with 2cm (¾-inch) fluted tube.
   Spread jam, then half the chocolate ganache on
   flat side of half the cooled pies; pipe whipped
   cream on top. Sandwich with remaining pies.
7 Spread remaining ganache over pies; sprinkle
   with coconut.

CHOCOLATE GANACHE
Bring cream to the boil in a small saucepan.
Remove from heat; add chocolate, stir until smooth.

You can use just one 300ml carton of thickened
cream for this recipe.
Whoopie pies are best eaten the day they are made.

RASPBERRY CHOCOLATE
Whoopie Pies

PREP + COOK TIME *1 HOUR* MAKES *20*

125g (4 ounces) unsalted butter, softened
½ cup (110g) firmly packed light brown sugar
1 egg
¾ cup (110g) plain (all-purpose) flour
⅓ cup (35g) cocoa powder
¼ cup (35g) self-raising flour
1 teaspoon bicarbonate of soda (baking soda)
⅔ cup (160ml) buttermilk
125g (4 ounces) fresh raspberries, halved
20 raspberry lollies

RASPBERRY BUTTERCREAM

125g (4 ounces) unsalted butter, softened
1½ cups (240g) icing (confectioners') sugar
1 tablespoon milk
pink food colouring
2 tablespoons raspberry jam

CHOCOLATE GANACHE

¼ cup (60ml) pouring cream
180g (5½ ounces) dark eating (semi-sweet)
    chocolate, chopped finely

1 Preheat oven to 200°C/400°F. Grease oven trays; line with baking paper.

2 Beat butter, sugar and egg in a small bowl with an electric mixer until light and fluffy. Beat in sifted dry ingredients and buttermilk, on low speed, until mixture is smooth.

3 Drop level tablespoons of mixture about 5cm (2 inches) apart onto trays.

4 Bake pies about 10 minutes. Cool on trays.

5 Meanwhile, make raspberry buttercream, then chocolate ganache.

6 Spoon buttercream into a piping bag fitted with a 2cm (¾-inch) fluted tube. Pipe buttercream on flat side of half the cooled pies; top with halved fresh raspberries, cut-side facing up. Spoon half the chocolate ganache over raspberries, then sandwich with remaining pies.

7 Spread remaining ganache over pies; top with raspberry lollies.

RASPBERRY BUTTERCREAM
Beat butter in a small bowl with an electric mixer until light and fluffy. Beat in sifted icing sugar and milk. Tint pink with colouring; stir in jam.

CHOCOLATE GANACHE
Bring cream to the boil in a small saucepan. Remove from heat; add chocolate, stir until smooth.

Whoopie pies are best eaten the day they are made.

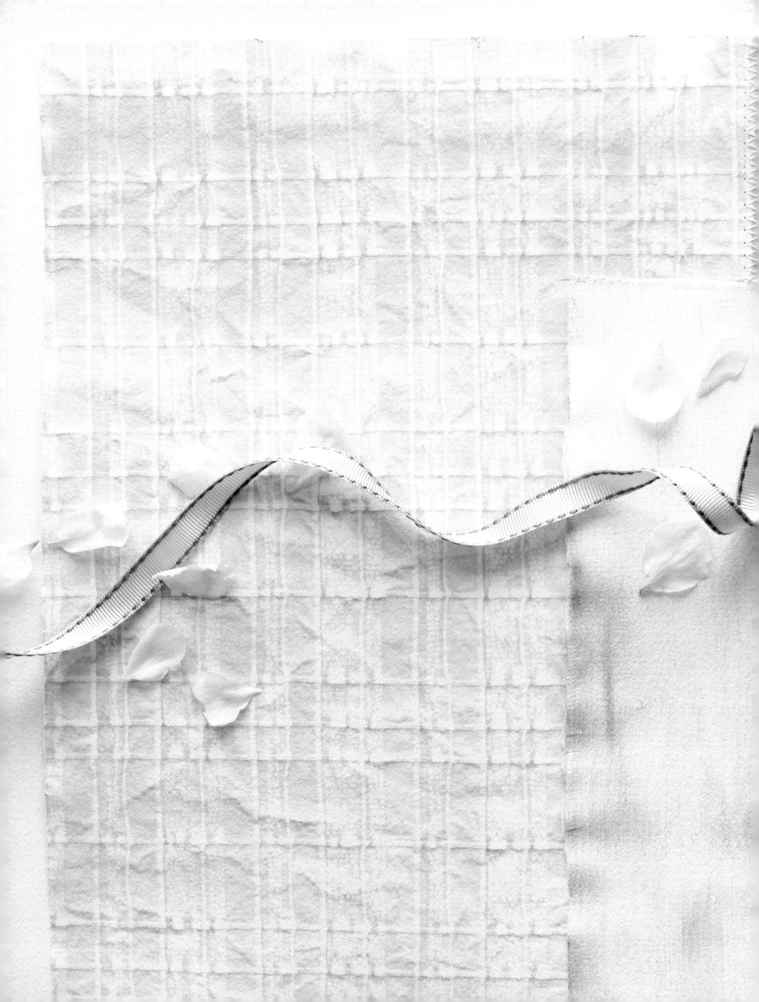

CHAPTER 5
PUDDINGS & PIES

CHOCOLATE FONDANTS
with Espresso Anglaise

PREP + COOK TIME *1 HOUR 15 MINUTES (+ REFRIGERATION)* MAKES *6*

150g (4½ ounces) butter, chopped
150g (4½ ounces) dark eating (semi-sweet)
 chocolate (70% cocoa), chopped coarsely
3 egg yolks
3 eggs
⅓ cup (75g) caster (superfine) sugar
⅔ cup (100g) plain (all-purpose) flour
2 teaspoons cocoa powder

ESPRESSO ANGLAISE

2 cups (500ml) milk
½ vanilla bean
4 egg yolks
2 tablespoons caster (superfine) sugar
2 tablespoons strong espresso coffee

1 Grease a 6-hole texas (¾-cup/180ml) muffin pan;
 line pan hole bases with rounds of baking paper.
2 Stir butter and chocolate in a medium saucepan
 over low heat until smooth. Transfer to a large bowl.
3 Beat egg yolks, eggs and sugar in a small bowl
 with an electric mixer until thick and creamy.
 Fold egg mixture and sifted flour into chocolate
 mixture. Spoon mixture into pan holes; place on
 an oven tray. Refrigerate 3 hours.
4 Make espresso anglaise.
5 Preheat oven to 180°C/350°F.
6 Bake fondants 14 minutes. Stand fondants 3 minutes.
 Use a small metal spatula to lever the fondants out
 of pan onto serving plates. Serve immediately with
 anglaise, dusted with cocoa powder.

ESPRESSO ANGLAISE

Bring milk to the boil in a small saucepan.
Meanwhile, scrape seeds from vanilla bean into a
medium heatproof bowl; add egg yolks and sugar,
whisk until combined. Gradually whisk hot milk
mixture into egg mixture; stir in coffee. Strain mixture
into the same pan; cook, stirring, over medium heat,
without boiling until mixture thickens and coats
the back of a wooden spoon. Strain mixture into
a medium bowl; stand bowl inside a larger bowl
filled with ice, stirring occasionally, until mixture
is cold.

It's important to have everything ready to go when
you're making the fondants. The cooking time is
critical – over-cooking will cook the centre of the
fondants right through, instead of them having a
lovely, silky, flowing centre. Make sure you work
quickly to remove the fondants from pan to plate –
and have the dessert-eaters ready and waiting.

CRÈME CARAMEL

PREP + COOK TIME *1 HOUR (+ REFRIGERATION)* **SERVES 8**

¾ cup (165g) caster (superfine) sugar
½ cup (125ml) water
6 eggs
1 teaspoon vanilla extract
½ cup (75g) caster (superfine) sugar, extra
1¼ cups (310ml) thickened (heavy) cream
  (see note)
1¾ cups (430ml) milk

1 Preheat oven to 160°C/325°F.
2 Stir sugar and the water in a medium heavy-based frying pan over heat, without boiling, until sugar dissolves. Bring to the boil; boil, uncovered, without stirring, until mixture is a deep caramel colour. Remove from heat; allow bubbles to subside. Pour toffee into a deep 20cm (8-inch) round cake pan.
3 Whisk eggs, extract and extra sugar in a large bowl.
4 Bring cream and milk to the boil in a medium saucepan. Whisking constantly, pour hot milk mixture into egg mixture. Strain mixture into a cake pan. Place pan in baking dish; add enough boiling water to come half way up side of pan.
5 Bake custard about 40 minutes or until set. Remove pan from baking dish. Cover; refrigerate overnight.
6 Gently ease crème caramel from side of pan; invert onto a deep-sided serving plate.

You can use just one 300ml carton of cream for this recipe.

WARM CHOCOLATE
and Caramel Puddings

PREP + COOK TIME *30 MINUTES* **MAKES 4**

125g (4 ounces) butter, softened
⅔ cup (150g) firmly packed light brown sugar
2 eggs
½ cup (75g) plain (all-purpose) flour
¼ cup (25g) cocoa powder
1½ tablespoons milk
12 caramel-filled chocolate squares

1 Preheat oven to 200°C/400°F. Grease four 1-cup (250ml) ovenproof dishes; line bases with baking paper.
2 Beat butter and sugar in a small bowl with an electric mixer until light and fluffy. Beat in eggs, one at a time. Stir in sifted flour, cocoa and milk.
3 Divide two-thirds of the mixture into dishes; place three caramel chocolate squares in centre of each mould. Spoon remaining mixture over chocolate squares; smooth surface.
4 Bake puddings about 20 minutes. Stand in dishes 10 minutes. Turn puddings onto serving plates; serve immediately.

SERVING SUGGESTION
Serve with thick (double) cream or ice-cream, dusted with sifted cocoa powder.

(PHOTOGRAPH PAGE 180)

WARM CHOCOLATE
and Caramel Puddings
(RECIPE PAGE 179)

PLUM COBBLER

(RECIPE PAGE 182)

PLUM COBBLER

PREP + COOK TIME *45 MINUTES* **SERVES 4**

825g (1¾ pounds) canned plums in syrup
¾ cup (110g) self-raising flour
¼ cup (55g) caster (superfine) sugar
1 teaspoon ground cinnamon
60g (2 ounces) butter, chopped coarsely
1 egg yolk
¼ cup (60ml) buttermilk, approximately
2 tablespoons coarsely chopped
   roasted hazelnuts
2 tablespoons icing (confectioners') sugar

1. Preheat oven to 180°C/350°F.
2. Drain plums over a medium saucepan. Halve plums; discard stones. Add plums to pan; bring to the boil. Reduce heat; simmer, uncovered, about 5 minutes or until plums soften.
3. Strain plums; reserve ½ cup liquid. Place plums and reserved liquid in a 1-litre (4-cup) ovenproof dish; place dish on an oven tray.
4. Sift flour, caster sugar and cinnamon into a medium bowl; rub in butter. Stir in egg yolk and enough of the buttermilk to make a soft, sticky dough. Drop heaped teaspoons of the mixture over hot plums; sprinkle with nuts.
5. Bake cobbler about 30 minutes or until browned lightly. Serve dusted with sifted icing sugar.

SERVING SUGGESTION
Serve with thick (double) cream or ice-cream.

(PHOTOGRAPH PAGE 181)

CHOCOLATE
Self-saucing Pudding

PREP + COOK TIME *50 MINUTES* **SERVES 6**

60g (2 ounces) butter
½ cup (125ml) milk
½ teaspoon vanilla extract
¾ cup (165g) caster (superfine) sugar
1 cup (150g) self-raising flour
1 tablespoon cocoa powder
¾ cup (165g) firmly packed light brown sugar
1 tablespoon cocoa powder, extra
2 cups (500ml) boiling water

1. Preheat oven to 180°C/350°F. Grease a 1.5 litre (6-cup) ovenproof dish.
2. Melt butter with milk in a medium saucepan. Remove from heat; stir in extract and caster sugar then sifted flour and cocoa. Spread mixture into dish. Sift brown sugar and extra cocoa over mixture; gently pour the boiling water over mixture.
3. Bake pudding about 40 minutes or until centre is firm. Stand 5 minutes before serving.

SERVING SUGGESTION
Serve with custard or cream.

CHOCOLATE
Self-saucing Pudding

BLUEBERRY APPLE CRUMBLE
Pie

PREP + COOK TIME *1 HOUR 10 MINUTES (+ REFRIGERATION)* SERVES *8*

1kg (2 pounds) apples
⅓ cup (75g) caster (superfine) sugar
⅔ cup (160ml) water
1½ tablespoons cornflour (cornstarch)
250g (8 ounces) fresh blueberries
½ cup (45g) rolled oats
½ teaspoon ground cinnamon
¼ cup (35g) plain (all-purpose) flour
¼ cup (55g) firmly packed light brown sugar
50g (1½ ounces) butter, chopped coarsely
⅓ cup (25g) flaked almonds

PASTRY
100g (3 ounces) butter, softened
2 tablespoons caster (superfine) sugar
1 egg yolk
1 cup (150g) plain (all-purpose) flour
½ cup (60g) ground almonds

1 Make pastry.
2 Peel, quarter and core apples; cut into 1cm (½-inch) pieces. Combine apple, caster sugar and ½ cup of the water in a large saucepan; cook, stirring, until sugar dissolves. Bring to the boil. Reduce heat; simmer, covered, 3 minutes. Uncover; simmer, about 2 minutes or until apple is tender. Stir in combined cornflour and the remaining water; cook, stirring, until mixture boils and thickens. Stir in blueberries. Remove from heat. Cool.
3 Preheat oven to 200°C/400°F.
4 Roll pastry between sheets of baking paper until large enough to line a deep 24cm (9½-inch) round loose-based fluted flan tin. Ease pastry into tin, press into base and side; trim edge. Place tin on an oven tray; refrigerate 20 minutes.
5 Line pastry with baking paper; fill with dried beans or rice. Bake 15 minutes. Remove paper and beans; bake about 10 minutes or until browned lightly.
6 Meanwhile, to make crumble mixture, combine oats, cinnamon, flour and brown sugar in a medium bowl; rub in butter. Stir in nuts.
7 Spoon apple mixture into pastry case; top with crumble mixture.
8 Bake pie about 35 minutes. Stand 15 minutes before serving.

PASTRY
Beat butter, sugar and egg yolk in a small bowl with an electric mixer until combined. Stir in sifted flour and ground almonds. Knead dough on a floured surface until smooth. Enclose pastry in plastic wrap; refrigerate 30 minutes.

SERVING SUGGESTION
Serve with whipped cream or ice-cream.

FIG AND RASPBERRY
Clafoutis

PREP + COOK TIME *50 MINUTES* **SERVES 6**

4 eggs
1 teaspoon vanilla bean paste
½ cup (110g) caster (superfine) sugar
½ cup (75g) plain (all-purpose) flour
2 cups (500ml) pouring cream
3 medium fresh figs (180g), cut into wedges
125g (4 ounces) fresh raspberries
1 tablespoon demerara sugar
2 teaspoons icing (confectioners') sugar

1 Preheat oven to 180°C/350°F. Grease a shallow
   2-litre (8-cup) ovenproof dish.
2 Whisk eggs, paste, caster sugar and flour in a
   medium bowl until smooth. Add cream; whisk to
   combine. Pour mixture into dish.
3 Arrange figs and raspberries over mixture; sprinkle
   with demerara sugar.
4 Bake clafoutis about 40 minutes. Stand 10 minutes
   before serving. Dust with sifted icing sugar.

SERVING SUGGESTION
Serve with whipped cream.

RHUBARB AND STRAWBERRY
Sponge Puddings

PREP + COOK TIME *1 HOUR* **MAKES 8**

5 cups (700g) coarsely chopped, trimmed rhubarb
2 tablespoons caster (superfine) sugar
2 tablespoons orange juice
500g (1 pound) strawberries, sliced thinly
SPONGE MIXTURE
2 eggs
½ cup (110g) caster (superfine) sugar
½ cup (75g) self-raising flour
½ tablespoon cornflour (cornstarch)

1 Preheat oven to 180°C/350°F.
2 Cook rhubarb, sugar and juice in a large saucepan
   over low heat, stirring, until sugar dissolves. Cook,
   uncovered, about 10 minutes or until rhubarb is
   tender. Stir in strawberries.
3 Meanwhile, make sponge mixture.
4 Spoon fruit mixture into eight 1-cup (250ml)
   ovenproof dishes; bake about 5 minutes or until
   fruit mixture is bubbling hot.
5 Top hot rhubarb mixture evenly with sponge mixture;
   bake about 30 minutes. Serve immediately.

SPONGE MIXTURE
Beat eggs in a small bowl with an electric mixer
about 10 minutes or until thick and creamy.
Gradually add sugar, beating until sugar dissolves.
Fold triple-sifted flours into egg mixture.

You need about 10 stems of rhubarb for this recipe.

SERVING SUGGESTION
Serve with custard or cream.

(PHOTOGRAPH PAGE 188)

RHUBARB AND STRAWBERRY
Sponge Puddings
(RECIPE PAGE 187)

APPLE AND MARMALADE
Streusel Puddings

(RECIPE PAGE 190)

APPLE AND MARMALADE
Streusel Puddings

PREP + COOK TIME *40 MINUTES (+ FREEZING)* SERVES *4*

4 medium apples (600g)
20g (¾ ounce) butter
2 tablespoons water
1 tablespoon caster (superfine) sugar
½ cup (170g) orange marmalade
2 teaspoons icing (confectioners') sugar

STREUSEL
½ cup (75g) plain (all-purpose) flour
¼ cup (35g) self-raising flour
⅓ cup (75g) firmly packed light brown sugar
½ teaspoon ground cinnamon
100g (3 ounces) butter, chopped

1 Make streusel.
2 Preheat oven to 200°C/400°F. Grease four ¾-cup (180ml) ovenproof dishes.
3 Peel and core apples, then thinly slice.
4 Melt butter in a medium frying pan; cook apple, the water and sugar, stirring, about 10 minutes or until apple is tender. Stir in marmalade. Spoon mixture into dishes.
5 Coarsely grate streusel onto a sheet of baking paper; sprinkle over apple mixture.
6 Bake puddings about 20 minutes or until browned lightly. Dust with sifted icing sugar before serving.

STREUSEL
Blend or process ingredients until combined. Roll into a ball. Enclose in plastic wrap; freeze 1 hour or until firm.

The cooked apple mixture can be stored, covered, in the fridge overnight. Streusel can be frozen for up to a week.

(PHOTOGRAPH PAGE 189)

HAZELNUT AND RAISIN BREAD
and Butter Pudding

PREP + COOK TIME *1 HOUR 15 MINUTES (+ STANDING)* SERVES *8*

¾ cup (100g) hazelnuts
2 cups (500ml) pouring cream
1½ cups (375ml) milk
350g (11 ounces) ciabatta bread
50g (1½ ounces) butter, melted
½ cup (85g) raisins
4 eggs
⅔ cup (150g) caster (superfine) sugar
½ teaspoon vanilla extract

1 Preheat oven to 180°C/350°F.
2 Place nuts on an oven tray; bake about 8 minutes or until skins begin to split. Place nuts in a tea towel and rub to remove skins. Chop nuts coarsely.
3 Bring cream, milk and hazelnuts to the boil in a medium saucepan. Remove from heat; cover, stand 20 minutes.
4 Remove crust from base of bread. Cut bread into 1.5cm (¾-inch) thick slices; brush one side of each slice with butter. Arrange bread, butter-side up, overlapping slightly, in a shallow 2-litre (8-cup) ovenproof dish; sprinkle raisins between layers.
5 Whisk eggs, sugar and extract in a large bowl until combined. Gradually whisk cream mixture into the egg mixture. Strain mixture into a jug; reserve nuts. Pour hot milk mixture over bread; sprinkle with reserved nuts.
6 Place dish in a large baking dish; add enough boiling water to baking dish to come halfway up sides of dish.
7 Bake pudding about 50 minutes or until set. Stand 10 minutes before serving.

BERRY AND RHUBARB
Pies

PREP + COOK TIME *1 HOUR 10 MINUTES (+ REFRIGERATION)* MAKES *6*

2 cups (220g) coarsely chopped rhubarb
¼ cup (55g) caster (superfine) sugar
2 tablespoons water
1 tablespoon cornflour (cornstarch)
2 cups (300g) frozen mixed berries
1 egg white
2 teaspoons caster (superfine) sugar, extra

PASTRY
1⅔ cups (250g) plain (all-purpose) flour
⅓ cup (75g) caster (superfine) sugar
150g (4½ ounces) cold butter, chopped
1 egg yolk
2 teaspoons iced water

1 Make pastry.
2 Place rhubarb, sugar and half the water in a medium saucepan; bring to the boil. Reduce heat; simmer, covered, about 3 minutes or until rhubarb is tender. Blend cornflour with the remaining water; stir into rhubarb mixture. Stir over heat until mixture boils and thickens. Remove from heat; stir in berries. Cool.
3 Grease 6-hole texas (¾-cup/180ml) muffin pan. Roll two-thirds of the pastry between sheets of baking paper until 5mm (¼ inch) thick; cut out six 12cm (4¾-inch) rounds. Press rounds into pan holes. Refrigerate 30 minutes.
4 Preheat oven to 200°C/400°F.
5 Roll remaining pastry between sheets of baking paper until 5mm (¼ inch) thick; cut out six 9cm (3¾-inch) rounds.

6 Spoon fruit mixture into pastry cases.
7 Brush edge of 9cm (3¾-inch) rounds with egg white; place over filling. Press edges firmly to seal. Brush tops with egg white; sprinkle with extra sugar.
8 Bake pies about 30 minutes. Stand in pan 10 minutes; using palette knife, loosen pies from edge of pan before lifting out. Serve warm.

PASTRY
Process flour, sugar and butter until crumbly. Add egg yolk and the water; process until combined. Knead dough on a floured surface until smooth. Enclose pastry in plastic wrap; refrigerate 30 minutes.

You need four large stems of rhubarb for this recipe.

SERVING SUGGESTION
Serve with vanilla ice-cream.

VARIATION

APPLE AND BLACKBERRY PIES Omit rhubarb and replace with 2 peeled, coarsely chopped medium apples. Cook with sugar and the water for about 5 minutes or until apples are just tender. Omit mixed berries and replace with 150g (4½ ounces) blackberries.

OLD-FASHIONED
Apple and Rhubarb Pie

PREP + COOK TIME *4 HOURS (+ COOLING & REFRIGERATION)* SERVES *8*

5 large apples (1kg), sliced thickly
⅓ cup (75g) caster (superfine) sugar
½ cup (125ml) water
1 vanilla bean, split lengthways
500g (1 pound) trimmed rhubarb,
    chopped coarsely
1 tablespoon lemon juice
1 egg, beaten lightly
1 teaspoon white (granulated) sugar

ALMOND PASTRY
2½ cups (375g) plain (all-purpose) flour
½ cup (60g) ground almonds
1 cup (160g) icing (confectioners') sugar
250g (8 ounces) cold butter, chopped coarsely
2 egg yolks
1 tablespoon iced water

1 Combine apple, caster sugar, the water and one half of the vanilla bean in a large saucepan, cover; bring to the boil. Reduce heat; simmer about 10 minutes or until apple is tender. Stir in rhubarb, cover; simmer about 3 minutes or until rhubarb is soft. Drain well. Transfer apple mixture to a medium bowl; stir in juice. Cool.
2 Make almond pastry.
3 Preheat oven to 180°C/350°F.
4 Roll two thirds of the pastry between sheets of baking paper until large enough to line a deep 24cm (9½-inch) pie dish. Lift pastry into dish; press into base and side, trim edge then pinch pastry. Refrigerate 30 minutes.

5 Line pastry with baking paper; fill with dried beans or rice. Place on an oven tray; bake 15 minutes. Remove paper and beans; bake a further 15 minutes or until browned. Cool.
6 Spoon apple mixture into pastry case. Roll the remaining pastry between sheets of baking paper until large enough to cover pie dish. Brush edge of pastry case with egg. Place pastry over pie; trim edge then pinch pastry. Cut out a 2.5cm (1-inch) round from centre of pie. Brush pastry with egg; sprinkle with white sugar.
7 Bake pie about 35 minutes or until browned. Stand 10 minutes before serving.

ALMOND PASTRY
Scrape seeds from remaining half of vanilla bean. Process flour, ground almonds, icing sugar and butter until crumbly. Add egg yolks, vanilla seeds and enough of the water, processing until ingredients just come together. Knead on a floured surface until smooth. Enclose pastry with plastic wrap; refrigerate 30 minutes.

SERVING SUGGESTION
Serve with whipped cream, ice-cream or custard.

LITTLE SALTY CARAMEL
Meringue Pies

PREP + COOK TIME 1 HOUR (+ REFRIGERATION) MAKES 8

395g (12½ ounces) canned sweetened
    condensed milk
30g (1 ounce) butter
¼ cup (90g) golden syrup or treacle
2 teaspoons sea salt flakes
¼ cup (60ml) pouring cream

PASTRY
1 cup (150g) plain (all-purpose) flour
⅓ cup (55g) icing (confectioners') sugar
90g (3 ounces) butter, chopped
1 egg yolk
1 tablespoon iced water, approximately

MERINGUE
4 egg whites
1 cup (220g) caster (superfine) sugar

1   Make pastry.
2   Grease eight 8cm (3-inch) round loose-based fluted flan tins. Divide pastry into eight portions. Roll a portion of pastry at a time between sheets of baking paper until large enough to line tins. Ease pastry into tins, press into sides; trim edges. Prick bases with fork. Place on an oven tray; refrigerate 20 minutes.
3   Meanwhile, preheat oven to 180°C/350°F.
4   Line pastry with baking paper; fill with dried beans or rice. Bake 10 minutes; remove paper and beans. Bake about 5 minutes or until browned; cool.
5   Stir condensed milk, butter, syrup and salt in a small heavy-based saucepan, over medium heat, about 12 minutes or until caramel-coloured. Stir in cream. Spread filling into pastry cases.
6   Make meringue; spoon meringue onto tarts.
7   Bake tarts about 5 minutes or until browned lightly. Stand 20 minutes before serving.

PASTRY
Process flour, icing sugar and butter until crumbly. Add egg yolk and enough of the water, processing until ingredients just come together. Knead dough on a floured surface until smooth. Enclose pastry with plastic wrap; refrigerate 30 minutes.

MERINGUE
Beat egg whites in a small bowl with an electric mixer until soft peaks form. Gradually add sugar, beating until sugar dissolves.

TRIPLE-CHOC
Pecan Pie

PREP + COOK TIME *1 HOUR 30 MINUTES (+ REFRIGERATION)* **SERVES 6**

1¾ cups (210g) pecan nuts

30g (1 ounce) dark eating (semi-sweet)
  chocolate, chopped coarsely

30g (1 ounce) milk eating chocolate,
  chopped coarsely

30g (1 ounce) white eating chocolate,
  chopped coarsely

50g (1½ ounces) butter, melted

1 cup (220g) firmly packed light brown sugar

2 tablespoons cornflour (cornstarch)

2 eggs

1 teaspoon vanilla extract

PASTRY

1½ cups (225g) plain (all-purpose) flour

2 tablespoons icing (confectioners') sugar

125g (4 ounces) cold butter, chopped coarsely

1 egg yolk

2 tablespoons iced water, approximately

1 Make pastry.

2 Grease a 12.5cm x 35cm (5-inch x 14-inch)
  rectangular loose-based fluted flan tin. Roll pastry
  between sheets of baking paper until large enough
  to line tin. Ease pastry into tin, press into side;
  trim edges. Refrigerate 30 minutes.

3 Preheat oven to 180°C/350°F.

4 Place tin on an oven tray. Line pastry case with
  baking paper; fill with dried beans or rice. Bake
  15 minutes. Remove paper and beans; bake about
  5 minutes or until browned lightly. Cool.

5 Reduce oven to 160°C/325°F.

6 Coarsely chop 1½ cups of the nuts; place in pastry
  case with all the chocolate. Whisk butter, sugar,
  cornflour, eggs and extract in a large bowl. Pour egg
  mixture into pastry case; top with remaining nuts.

7 Bake pie about 35 minutes or until filling is set.
  Cool before serving.

PASTRY

Process flour, sugar and butter until crumbly. Add
egg yolk and enough of the water, processing until
ingredients come together. Knead dough on floured
surface until smooth. Enclose pastry in plastic wrap;
refrigerate 30 minutes.

Store leftover pie in an airtight container for up
to three days.

PEAR AND CINNAMON SUGAR
Lattice Pies

PREP + COOK TIME *1 HOUR 15 MINUTES (+ REFRIGERATION)* **MAKES** *4*

3 large pears (990g), peeled, cored, sliced thinly
¼ cup (55g) caster (superfine) sugar
2 teaspoons cornflour (cornstarch)
1 teaspoon vanilla extract
1 egg white
½ teaspoon ground cinnamon

PASTRY

1½ cups (225g) plain (all-purpose) flour
2 tablespoons icing (confectioners') sugar
125g (4 ounces) cold butter, chopped
1 egg yolk
2 tablespoons iced water, approximately

1 Make pastry.
2 Grease four 10cm (4-inch) round loose-based
   fluted flan tins. Divide pastry into five portions.
   Roll one of four portions of pastry at a time
   between sheets of baking paper until large enough
   to line tins. Ease pastry into tins, press into sides;
   trim edges. Reserve pastry scraps, adding them to
   the fifth portion. Refrigerate 30 minutes.
3 Preheat oven to 180°C/350°F.
4 Meanwhile, cook pear and one-third of the sugar in
   a medium saucepan, covered, until pear is tender.
   Drain; reserve 1 tablespoon liquid. Blend or process
   pear mixture until almost smooth. Return to pan
   with half the remaining sugar. Blend cornflour with
   reserved liquid, stir into pear mixture; cook, stirring,
   until mixture boils and thickens. Stir in extract; cool.
5 Spoon pear filling into pastry cases. Brush edges
   with egg white. Roll all reserved pastry between
   sheets of baking paper until 5mm (¼-inch) thick.
   Cut into 12 x 1cm (½-inch) strips. Weave strips over
   pies. Trim edges, pressing to seal; sprinkle with
   combined remaining sugar and cinnamon.
6 Bake pies about 50 minutes or until browned lightly.
   Stand 20 minutes before removing pies from tins.
   Serve warm or at room temperature.

PASTRY

Process flour, sugar and butter until crumbly. Add
egg yolk and enough of the water, processing until
ingredients just come together. Knead dough on
a floured surface until smooth. Enclose pastry in
plastic wrap; refrigerate 30 minutes.

SERVING SUGGESTION

Serve with cream or ice-cream.

CHOCOLATE HAZELNUT
Pie

PREP + COOK TIME *1 HOUR 30 MINUTES (+ REFRIGERATION)* SERVES *10*

1½ cups (210g) hazelnuts
¾ cup (165g) firmly packed light brown sugar
100g (3 ounces) butter
1 teaspoon vanilla extract
1 cup (250ml) pouring cream
150g (4½ ounces) dark eating (semi-sweet)
  chocolate, chopped coarsely

PASTRY

1½ cups (225g) plain (all-purpose) flour
2 tablespoons icing (confectioners') sugar
125g (4 ounces) cold butter, chopped
1 egg yolk
2 tablespoons iced water, approximately

1 Make pastry.
2 Grease a 24cm (9½-inch) round loose-based fluted flan tin. Roll pastry between sheets of baking paper until large enough to line tin. Ease pastry into tin, press into base and side; trim edge. Cover; refrigerate 30 minutes.
3 Preheat oven to 180°C/350°F.
4 Place tin on an oven tray. Line pastry case with baking paper; fill with dried beans or rice. Bake 15 minutes. Remove paper and beans; bake about 15 minutes or until browned lightly. Cool.

5 Place nuts on an oven tray; roast about 5 minutes or until browned lightly, cool. Place nuts in a tea towel; rub to remove skins. Place nuts in pastry case.
6 Combine sugar, butter, extract and ⅔ cup cream in a small saucepan; bring to the boil. Reduce heat; simmer, uncovered, about 8 minutes or until golden and thickened. Pour caramel over nuts; cool until filling is firm.
7 Place chocolate in a small heatproof bowl. Bring remaining cream to the boil in a small saucepan. Pour hot cream over chocolate; stir until smooth. Spread chocolate mixture over pie. Refrigerate 3 hours or overnight. Remove pie from refrigerator 30 minutes before serving.

PASTRY

Process flour, sugar and butter until crumbly. Add egg yolk and enough of the water, processing until ingredients come together. Knead dough on a floured surface until smooth. Enclose pastry in plastic wrap; refrigerate 30 minutes.

Store leftover pie in an airtight container in the fridge for up to three days.

FIG CUSTARD TART

PREP + COOK TIME *1 HOUR 30 MINUTES (+ REFRIGERATION & COOLING)* **SERVES** *8*

250g (8 ounces) dried figs, chopped finely
½ cup (125ml) boiling water
2 tablespoons brandy
1 cup (250ml) pouring cream
3 eggs
⅔ cup (150g) caster (superfine) sugar
1 teaspoon vanilla extract

PASTRY

1¼ cups (175g) plain (all-purpose) flour
⅓ cup (55g) icing (confectioners') sugar
¼ cup (30g) ground almonds
125g (4 ounces) cold butter, chopped
1 egg yolk
1 teaspoon iced water

1 Make pastry.

2 Grease a 24cm (9½-inch) round loose-based fluted flan tin. Roll pastry between sheets of baking paper until large enough to line tin. Lift pastry into tin; press into side, trim edge. Refrigerate 20 minutes.

3 Preheat oven to 200°C/400°F.

4 Place tin on an oven tray, line pastry case with baking paper; fill with dried beans or rice. Bake 10 minutes. Remove paper and beans; bake about 8 minutes or until pastry is browned lightly. Cool.

5 Reduce oven to 150°C/300°F.

6 Meanwhile, place figs and the water in a small saucepan; bring to the boil. Reduce heat; simmer, uncovered, about 5 minutes or until mixture is thick and pulpy. Remove from heat; stir in brandy. Blend or process fig mixture until smooth; spread into pastry case.

7 Bring cream to the boil in a small saucepan; remove from heat. Whisk eggs, sugar and extract in a medium bowl until combined. Gradually whisk hot cream mixture into egg mixture; pour custard into pastry case.

8 Bake tart about 20 minutes or until custard sets. Cool 10 minutes. Using a blowtorch, caramelise top of tart. Cool in tin.

PASTRY

Process flour, icing sugar, ground almonds and butter until crumbly. Add egg yolk and the water; process until ingredients come together. Knead dough on a floured surface until smooth. Enclose pastry in plastic wrap; refrigerate 30 minutes.

Blowtorches are available from kitchenware and hardware stores.
Store leftover tart in an airtight container in the fridge for up to two days.

SERVING SUGGESTION

Serve with thick (double) cream; dust with sifted icing sugar.

CARAMEL APPLE
Streusel Pies

PREP + COOK TIME *55 MINUTES (+ REFRIGERATION & FREEZING)* **MAKES** *12*

⅓ cup (50g) self-raising flour
⅓ cup (50g) plain (all-purpose) flour
⅓ cup (75g) firmly packed light brown sugar
½ teaspoon ground cinnamon
80g (2½ ounces) cold butter, chopped
400g (12½ ounces) canned pie apple
2 tablespoons golden syrup or treacle
1 tablespoon pouring cream
2 teaspoons icing (confectioners') sugar

PASTRY
1¼ cups (185g) plain (all-purpose) flour
¼ cup (55g) firmly packed light brown sugar
125g (4 ounces) butter, chopped
1 egg yolk
2 teaspoons iced water, approximately

1 Make pastry.
2 Grease a 12-hole (⅓-cup/80ml) muffin pan. Roll
   pastry between sheets of baking paper until 5mm
   (¼-inch) thick. Cut 12 x 8cm (3¼-inch) rounds from
   pastry; press rounds into pan holes. Prick base of
   cases well with fork. Refrigerate 30 minutes.
3 Preheat oven to 180°C/350°F.
4 Bake pastry cases about 12 minutes. Cool.
5 Meanwhile, to make streusel topping, process
   flours, sugar, cinnamon and butter until combined.
   Roll dough into a ball, enclose in plastic wrap;
   freeze about 15 minutes or until firm.
6 Combine apple, golden syrup and cream in a
   medium bowl; spoon mixture into pastry cases.
   Coarsely grate streusel topping over apple mixture.
7 Bake pies about 25 minutes. Stand 10 minutes
   before serving; dust with icing sugar.

PASTRY
Process flour, sugar and butter until crumbly. Add
egg yolk and enough of the water, processing
until ingredients come together. Knead dough on
a floured surface until smooth. Enclose pastry in
plastic wrap; refrigerate 30 minutes.

LEMON MERINGUE
Pie

PREP + COOK TIME *1 HOUR 10 MINUTES (+ REFRIGERATION)* **SERVES** *10*

½ cup (75g) cornflour (cornstarch)
1 cup (220g) caster (superfine) sugar
½ cup (125ml) lemon juice
1¼ cups (310ml) water
2 teaspoons finely grated lemon rind
60g (2 ounces) unsalted butter, chopped
3 eggs, separated
½ cup (110g) caster (superfine) sugar, extra

PASTRY

1½ cups (225g) plain (all-purpose) flour
1 tablespoon icing (confectioners') sugar
140g (4½ ounces) cold butter, chopped
1 egg yolk
2 tablespoons cold water

1   Make pastry.
2   Grease a 24cm (9½-inch) round loose-based fluted flan tin. Roll pastry between sheets of baking paper until large enough to line tin. Ease pastry into tin, press into base and side; trim edge. Cover; refrigerate 30 minutes.
3   Preheat oven to 240°C/475°F.
4   Place tin on an oven tray. Line pastry case with baking paper; fill with dried beans or rice. Bake 15 minutes; remove paper and beans. Bake about 10 minutes; cool. Turn oven off.

5   Meanwhile, combine cornflour and sugar in a medium saucepan; gradually stir in juice and the water until smooth. Cook, stirring, until mixture boils and thickens. Reduce heat; simmer, stirring, 1 minute. Remove from heat; stir in rind, butter and egg yolks. Cool 10 minutes.
6   Spread filling into pie shell. Cover; refrigerate 2 hours.
7   Preheat oven to 240°C/475°F.
8   Beat egg whites in a small bowl with an electric mixer until soft peaks form; gradually add extra sugar, beating until sugar dissolves.
9   Roughen surface of filling with a fork before spreading with meringue mixture. Bake pie about 2 minutes or until meringue is browned lightly.

PASTRY

Process flour, sugar and butter until crumbly. Add egg yolk and the water; process until ingredients come together. Knead dough on a floured surface until smooth. Enclose pastry with plastic wrap; refrigerate 30 minutes.

This pie is best eaten on the day it is made.

CHAPTER 6
BREADS
& BUNS

DINNER ROLLS

PREP + COOK TIME *45 MINUTES (+ STANDING)* **MAKES** *20*

2 teaspoons (7g) dried yeast
1 teaspoon caster (superfine) sugar
2 cups (500ml) warm water
4 cups (640g) baker's flour (see notes)
2 teaspoons salt
cooking-oil spray

1 Whisk yeast, sugar and the water in a medium jug until yeast dissolves. Cover; stand in a warm place about 15 minutes or until mixture is frothy.

2 Sift flour and salt into a large bowl; stir in yeast mixture. Turn dough onto a floured surface; knead about 15 minutes or until dough is smooth and elastic. Place dough in an oiled large bowl, turning dough once to coat in oil. Cover; stand in a warm place about 1 hour or until dough doubles in size.

3 Preheat oven to 200°C/400°F. Oil oven trays.

4 Knead dough on a floured surface about 1 minute or until smooth. Divide dough into quarters; divide each quarter into five pieces.

5 Shape each piece of dough into a ball; place balls, 5cm (2 inches) apart, on trays. Cut a small cross in top of each ball; coat lightly with cooking-oil spray. Cover loosely with plastic wrap; stand in a warm place about 20 minutes or until dough doubles in size.

6 Bake rolls about 15 minutes or until they sound hollow when tapped. Transfer to a wire rack to cool.

16

If you can't get baker's flour you can use regular supermarket-standard plain (all-purpose) flour. Baker's flour will give you a more memorable result though. It is much stronger than regular plain flour – it contains more gluten – and so, will produce a good crust on these rolls. The same goes for bread.

These rolls are best eaten on the day they are made. They can be frozen for up to three months.

SPINACH AND FETTA
Damper

PREP + COOK TIME *1 HOUR 10 MINUTES (+ STANDING)* SERVES *8*

1 tablespoon olive oil
1 medium white onion (150g), chopped finely
300g (9½ ounces) baby spinach leaves
1 tablespoon fresh thyme leaves
1 tablespoon finely chopped fresh rosemary
2 cups (300g) self-raising flour
½ cup (80g) wholemeal self-raising flour
50g (1½ ounces) cold butter, chopped coarsely
1 cup (120g) coarsely grated parmesan cheese
1 cup (250ml) buttermilk
1 egg
60g (2 ounces) danish fetta cheese, crumbled

1 Heat oil in a large frying pan; cook onion, stirring, until softened. Add washed, drained (not dried) spinach; cook, stirring, until wilted. Remove from heat; when cool enough to handle, squeeze out excess liquid. Combine spinach and herbs in a medium bowl; season.

2 Preheat oven to 200°C/400°F. Line a large oven tray with baking paper.

3 Sift flours into a large bowl; rub in butter. Stir in half the parmesan. Make a well in the centre; stir in combined buttermilk and egg, mix to a soft, sticky dough.

4 Knead dough gently on a floured surface until smooth. Press dough into a 20cm x 30cm (8-inch x 12-inch) rectangle. Spread spinach mixture over dough leaving 2cm (¾-inch) strip along one long side. Sprinkle remaining parmesan and fetta over spinach. Roll up firmly, from the other long side; place on tray.

5 Using a sharp knife, cut the top of dough to make eight slices, without cutting all the way through. Brush with a little extra buttermilk.

6 Bake damper about 40 minutes or until loaf sounds hollow when tapped. Stand damper 30 minutes before serving.

This damper is best eaten on the day it is made – even better eaten warm.

CRUSTY SEED ROLLS

PREP + COOK TIME *1 HOUR 20 MINUTES (+ STANDING)* **MAKES** *12*

3 teaspoons (10g) dried yeast
¾ cup (180ml) warm water
2 teaspoons caster (superfine) sugar
2 cups (300g) white plain (all-purpose) flour
½ cup (75g) wholemeal plain (all-purpose) flour
1 teaspoon salt
30g (1 ounce) butter, melted
½ cup (125ml) warm milk
¼ cup (50g) pepitas (pumpkin seeds)
¼ cup (35g) sunflower seeds
1 tablespoon linseeds
1 egg yolk, beaten lightly
2 tablespoons pepitas (pumpkin seeds), extra
2 tablespoons sunflower seeds, extra
1 tablespoon linseeds, extra
1 teaspoon salt, extra

1 Whisk yeast, water and sugar in a small bowl until yeast dissolves. Cover; stand in a warm place about 10 minutes or until frothy.
2 Sift flours and salt into a large bowl; stir in yeast mixture, butter, milk and seeds. Knead dough on a floured surface about 5 minutes or until smooth and elastic. Transfer to an oiled large bowl. Cover; stand in a warm place about 1 hour or until dough has doubled in size.
3 Punch down dough; knead on a floured surface until smooth. Divide dough into 12 portions; shape each portion into a round roll. Place on an oiled oven tray, cover; stand in warm place about 15 minutes or until doubled in size.
4 Preheat oven to 200°C/400°F.
5 Using a sharp knife, slash the top of each roll. Brush rolls with egg yolk; sprinkle with extra seeds and salt, pressing down lightly.
6 Bake rolls about 25 minutes or until they sound hollow when tapped.

These rolls are best eaten on the day they are made. They can be frozen for up to three months.

DAMPER

PREP + COOK TIME *45 MINUTES* SERVES *6*

3 cups (450g) self-raising flour
30g (1 ounce) butter
½ cup (125ml) milk
1 cup (250ml) water, approximately

1 Preheat oven to 180°C/350°F. Oil an oven tray.
2 Sift flour into a large bowl; rub in butter. Make a well in centre; add milk and enough water to mix to a soft, sticky dough.
3 Knead dough on a floured surface until smooth. Press dough into a 15cm (6-inch) circle, place on tray. Score dough, about 1cm (½ inch) deep. Brush top with a little extra milk or water; dust with a little extra flour.
4 Bake damper about 30 minutes or until damper sounds hollow when tapped. Stand 10 minutes before serving.

SERVING SUGGESTION
Serve with butter and golden syrup.

BASIC TURKISH PIDE

PREP + COOK TIME *30 MINUTES (+ STANDING)* SERVES *8*

2 teaspoons (7g) dried yeast
1 teaspoon caster (superfine) sugar
⅔ cup (160ml) warm water
2 tablespoons warm milk
2 cups (300g) plain (all-purpose) flour
1 teaspoon salt
2 tablespoons olive oil
2 teaspoons black sesame seeds

1 Whisk yeast, sugar, the water and milk in a small jug until yeast dissolves; stand in warm place about 10 minutes or until frothy.
2 Place ½ cup of the flour in a large bowl; whisk in yeast mixture. Cover; stand in a warm place 1 hour.
3 Stir remaining sifted flour, salt and half the oil into yeast mixture. Knead dough on a floured surface until smooth. Place in an oiled large bowl, cover; stand in a warm place about 1 hour or until dough has doubled in size.
4 Preheat oven to 240°C/475°F. Heat an oven tray.
5 Roll dough into a 35cm (14-inch) oval shape; place on baking paper. Make indents with your finger, then brush with remaining oil; sprinkle with sesame seeds. Lift dough on paper onto the heated oven tray.
6 Bake pide about 15 minutes or until it sounds hollow when tapped.

Pide is best made on the day of serving.

(PHOTOGRAPH PAGE 222)

BASIC TURKISH PIDE

(RECIPE PAGE 221)

OLIVE BREAD

(RECIPE PAGE 224)

OLIVE BREAD

PREP + COOK TIME *1 HOUR 45 MINUTES (+ STANDING)* SERVES *12*

2 teaspoons (7g) dried yeast
1 teaspoon caster (superfine) sugar
1¼ cups (310ml) warm milk
3⅓ cups (500g) plain (all-purpose) flour
1 teaspoon salt
¼ cup (60ml) extra virgin olive oil
1 cup (120g) seeded black olives,
    chopped finely

1 Whisk yeast, sugar and milk in small jug until yeast dissolves; stand in a warm place about 15 minutes or until mixture is frothy.
2 Sift flour and salt into a large bowl. Stir in yeast mixture and oil; mix to a firm dough. Knead dough on a floured surface about 5 minutes or until smooth and elastic. Place dough in an oiled large bowl, cover; stand in a warm place about 1½ hours or until dough has doubled in size.
3 Knead dough onto a floured surface until smooth. Press dough into a 23cm x 28cm (9¼-inch x 11¼-inch) rectangle. Spread olives over dough, leaving 2cm (¾-inch) border. Roll up dough from long side, tuck ends underneath; place on an oiled oven tray.
4 Sift a little extra flour over bread. Using scissors, make cuts about 2.5cm (1 inch) apart, along centre of bread. Place bread in a warm place; stand, uncovered, about 1 hour or until doubled in size.
5 Meanwhile, preheat oven to 180°C/350°F.
6 Bake bread about 1 hour or until it sounds hollow when tapped.

This bread is best made on day of serving.

(PHOTOGRAPH PAGE 223)

CHEESE AND

Olive Loaf

PREP + COOK TIME *50 MINUTES* SERVES *8*

1 cup (150g) self-raising flour
⅔ cup (80g) coarsely grated gruyère cheese
1 cup (120g) seeded green olives,
    chopped coarsely
75g (2½ ounces) ham, chopped coarsely
2 tablespoons coarsely chopped fresh mint
½ teaspoon ground black pepper
4 eggs, beaten lightly
80g (2½ ounces) butter, melted

1 Preheat oven to 200°C/400°F. Oil a 10.5cm x 21cm (4-inch x 8½-inch) loaf pan.
2 Sift flour into a medium bowl; add cheese, olives, ham, mint and pepper. Add egg and butter; stir until well combined. Spread mixture into pan.
3 Bake loaf about 35 minutes or until browned lightly. Turn onto a wire rack to cool.

This loaf is suitable to freeze for up to two months.

CHEESE AND
Olive Loaf

HOT CROSS BUNS

PREP + COOK TIME *1 HOUR 35 MINUTES (+ STANDING & COOLING)* **MAKES** *16*

4 teaspoons (14g) dried yeast
¼ cup (55g) caster (superfine) sugar
1½ cups (375ml) warm milk
4 cups (600g) plain (all-purpose) flour
1 teaspoon mixed spice
½ teaspoon ground cinnamon
60g (2 ounces) butter
1 egg
¾ cup (120g) sultanas

FLOUR PASTE

½ cup (75g) plain (all-purpose) flour
2 teaspoons caster (superfine) sugar
⅓ cup (80ml) water, approximately

GLAZE

1 tablespoon caster (superfine) sugar
1 teaspoon gelatine
1 tablespoon water

1 Whisk yeast, sugar and milk in a small bowl or jug until yeast dissolves. Cover; stand in a warm place about 10 minutes or until mixture is frothy.

2 Sift flour and spices into a large bowl; rub in butter. Stir in yeast mixture, egg and sultanas; mix to a soft, sticky dough. Cover; stand in a warm place about 45 minutes or until dough has doubled in size.

3 Grease a deep 22cm (9-inch) square cake pan.

4 Knead dough on a floured surface about 5 minutes or until smooth and elastic. Divide dough into 16 pieces; knead into balls. Place balls into pan, cover; stand in a warm place about 10 minutes or until buns have risen two-thirds of the way up the pan.

5 Preheat oven to 220°C/425°F.

6 Make flour paste for crosses; place in a piping bag fitted with a small plain tube. Pipe crosses on buns.

7 Bake buns about 30 minutes or until they sound hollow when tapped. Turn buns, top-side up, onto a wire rack.

8 Make glaze; brush hot glaze on hot buns. Cool.

FLOUR PASTE

Combine flour and sugar in cup. Gradually blend in enough of the water to form a smooth firm paste.

GLAZE

Stir ingredients in a small saucepan over heat, without boiling, until sugar and gelatine are dissolved.

Buns are best made on the day of serving. Unglazed buns can be frozen for up to three months.

GRAIN AND SEED LOAF

PREP + COOK TIME *1 HOUR 10 MINUTES (+ STANDING)* **MAKES** *18 SLICES*

1 cup (160g) burghul
3 teaspoons (10g) dried yeast
1 teaspoon caster (superfine) sugar
¾ cup (180ml) warm milk
¼ cup (60ml) warm water
2¼ cups (335g) white plain (all-purpose) flour
½ cup (80g) wholemeal plain (all-purpose) flour
1 teaspoon salt
2 tablespoons linseeds
2 teaspoons olive oil
1 tablespoon milk, extra
1 tablespoon sesame seeds

1 Place burghul in a medium heatproof bowl, cover with boiling water. Cover; stand 30 minutes. Rinse well; drain well.

2 Whisk yeast, sugar, milk and the water in a small bowl until yeast dissolves. Cover; stand in a warm place about 10 minutes or until mixture is frothy.

3 Sift flours and salt into a large bowl, add burghul and linseeds. Stir in oil and yeast mixture; mix to a soft dough. Knead dough on a floured surface about 10 minutes or until dough is smooth and elastic. Place dough in a large oiled bowl; cover, stand in a warm place about 1 hour or until dough has doubled in size.

4 Preheat oven to 220°C/425°F. Oil a 14cm x 21cm (5½-inch x 8½-inch) loaf pan.

5 Punch down dough. Knead dough on a floured surface until smooth. Divide dough into three pieces. Shape each piece into a 30cm (12-inch) sausage. Plait sausages together, place into pan. Cover; stand in a warm place about 30 minutes or until risen.

6 Brush dough with extra milk, sprinkle evenly with sesame seeds. Bake bread about 45 minutes or until it sounds hollow when tapped; turn onto a wire rack to cool.

This loaf can be frozen for up to three months.

ROTI

ROTI

PREP + COOK TIME *1 HOUR (+ REFRIGERATION)* **MAKES** *16*

1 cup (150g) white plain (all-purpose) flour
1 cup (160g) wholemeal plain (all-purpose) flour
1 teaspoon salt
1 teaspoon ground coriander
½ teaspoon ground turmeric
2 teaspoons cumin seeds
1 tablespoon vegetable oil
¾ cup (180ml) water, approximately
4 tablespoons ghee (clarified butter),
   approximately

1 Sift flours, salt and ground spices into a large bowl. Make a well in centre; add seeds, oil and enough water to mix to a soft dough. Knead dough on a floured surface 10 minutes. Enclose dough in plastic wrap; refrigerate 30 minutes.
2 Divide dough into 16 portions; roll each portion on a floured surface into a 16cm (6½-inch) round.
3 Heat a heavy-based frying pan until very hot; add about 1 teaspoon of the ghee, quickly tilt pan to coat base with ghee. Place one round into pan; cook about 1 minute or until round is puffed slightly and bubbles start to form. Turn; brown other side. Repeat with remaining ghee and rounds.

Roti and chapati are both made with a similar unleavened dough. The difference between them is that roti are fried in ghee and chapati are grilled or cooked over a direct flame. Watch the ghee when making these; when it begins to burn and a few roti have been cooked, wipe the pan clean with absorbent paper.
Roti are best made as close to serving time as possible.

BASIC WHITE BREAD

PREP + COOK TIME *1 HOUR 15 MINUTES (+ STANDING)*
MAKES *18 SLICES*

3 teaspoons (10g) dried yeast
⅔ cup (160ml) warm water
2 teaspoons caster (superfine) sugar
2½ cups (375g) plain (all-purpose) flour
1 teaspoon salt
30g (1 ounce) butter, melted
½ cup (125ml) warm milk

1 Whisk yeast, the water and sugar in a small bowl until yeast dissolves. Cover; stand in a warm place about 10 minutes or until mixture is frothy.
2 Sift flour and salt into a large bowl; stir in butter, milk and yeast mixture. Knead dough on a floured surface about 10 minutes or until dough is smooth and elastic. Place dough into an oiled large bowl, cover; stand in a warm place about 1 hour or until dough has doubled in size.
3 Preheat oven to 200°C/400°F. Oil a 10cm (4-inch) deep, 9cm x 15cm (3¼-inch x 6-inch) bread tin.
4 Knead dough on a floured surface until smooth. Divide dough in half. Roll each half into a ball; place side-by-side in bread tin. Dust with a little extra flour. Cover; stand in a warm place 20 minutes or until risen.
5 Bake bread about 45 minutes or until it sounds hollow when tapped. Turn onto a wire rack to cool.

Bread can be frozen for up to three months.

(PHOTOGRAPH PAGE 232)

BASIC WHITE BREAD

(RECIPE PAGE 231)

BAGUETTES
(French Bread Sticks)
(RECIPE PAGE 234)

BAGUETTES
(French Bread Sticks)

PREP + COOK TIME *1 HOUR (+ STANDING)*

MAKES 4 (EACH MAKES 20 SLICES)

3 teaspoons (10g) dried yeast
⅔ cup (160ml) warm water
2 teaspoons caster (superfine) sugar
2½ cups (375g) plain (all-purpose) flour
1 teaspoon salt
30g (1 ounce) butter, melted
½ cup (125ml) warm milk

1 Whisk yeast, water and sugar in a small bowl until yeast dissolves. Cover; stand in a warm place about 10 minutes or until frothy.
2 Sift flours and salt into a large bowl; stir in yeast mixture, butter and milk. Knead dough on a floured surface about 10 minutes or until smooth and elastic. Place in an oiled large bowl, cover; stand in a warm place about 1 hour or until dough has doubled in size.
3 Punch down dough; knead on a floured surface until smooth. Divide dough into four portions; shape each portion into a 40cm (16-inch) long sausage. Place on oiled oven trays, cover; stand in a warm place 15 minutes.
4 Preheat oven to 200°C/400°F.
5 Slash each baguette a few times, diagonally, with a sharp knife; brush with a little water.
6 Bake baguettes about 30 minutes or until they sound hollow when tapped.

These baguettes are best made on the day of serving.

(PHOTOGRAPH PAGE 233)

ZUCCHINI AND CORN
Bread

PREP + COOK TIME *2 HOURS 15 MINUTES* **SERVES 12**

1 medium zucchini (120g)
2 cups (300g) self-raising flour
1 teaspoon salt
1 cup (170g) polenta (cornmeal)
½ cup (60g) coarsely grated cheddar cheese
1 teaspoon dried chilli flakes
420g (13½ ounces) canned corn kernels,
    rinsed, drained
310g (10 ounces) canned creamed corn
½ cup (125ml) buttermilk
3 eggs
2 tablespoons pine nuts

1 Preheat oven to 180°C/350°F. Oil a 14cm x 23cm (5½-inch x 9¼-inch) loaf pan; line base and sides with baking paper.
2 Coarsely grate zucchini, place in a sieve; squeeze out excess water, drain well.
3 Sift flour and salt into a large bowl; stir in polenta, cheese and chilli. Stir in combined zucchini, corn kernels, creamed corn, buttermilk and eggs. Spread mixture into pan; sprinkle with nuts.
4 Bake bread about 2 hours (cover pan with foil if loaf is getting too brown). Stand bread in pan 5 minutes; turn, top-side up, onto a wire rack to cool.

This bread is best made on the day of serving.

ZUCCHINI AND CORN
Bread

HOT CROSS BUN
Scones

(RECIPE PAGE 238)

HOT CROSS BUN
Scones

PREP + COOK TIME *45 MINUTES (+ STANDING)* MAKES *28*

1 cup (160g) dried currants
2 tablespoons dark rum
3½ cups (525g) self-raising flour
2 teaspoons mixed spice
1 teaspoon ground cinnamon
1 cup (250ml) lemonade
1 cup (250ml) pouring cream
½ cup (80g) icing (confectioners') sugar
3 teaspoons lemon juice

1 Combine currants and rum in medium bowl. Cover; stand 2 hours.
2 Preheat oven to 220°/425°F. Grease a 20cm x 30cm (8-inch x 12-inch) rectangular pan.
3 Sift flour and spices into a large bowl. Make a well in centre; add lemonade, cream and currant mixture. Use a knife to "cut" the lemonade, cream and currants through the flour mixture, mixing to a soft, sticky dough. Knead dough gently on a floured surface until smooth.
4 Press dough out to 2.5cm (1 inch) thickness. Dip a 4cm (1½-inch) round cutter in flour; cut as many rounds as you can from dough. Place rounds, side-by-side, just touching, in pan. Gently knead scraps of dough together; repeat pressing and cutting of dough, place in same pan. Brush tops with a little extra cream.
5 Bake scones about 20 minutes or until browned lightly and scones sound hollow when tapped.
6 Combine sifted icing sugar and juice in a small bowl; spoon icing into a small piping bag fitted with a 5mm (¼-inch) plain tube. Pipe a cross onto each scone.

SERVING SUGGESTION
Serve warm scones with butter.

(PHOTOGRAPH PAGES 236 & 237)

COCONUT
Banana Bread

PREP + COOK TIME *1 HOUR 40 MINUTES (+ STANDING)* SERVES *10*

1⅓ cups (200g) self-raising flour
1 cup (150g) plain (all-purpose) flour
⅔ cup (150g) firmly packed light brown sugar
½ cup (40g) desiccated coconut
1½ cups mashed banana
3 eggs
⅔ cup (160ml) vegetable oil
1 teaspoon coconut essence
½ cup (25g) flaked coconut

1 Preheat oven to 180°C/350°F. Grease a 14cm x 21cm (5½-inch x 8½-inch) loaf pan; line base and sides with baking paper, extending the paper 5cm (2 inches) over sides.
2 Sift flours into a large bowl; stir in sugar, desiccated coconut and banana, then combined eggs, oil and essence until just combined. Spread mixture into pan; sprinkle flaked coconut on top, pressing down lightly.
3 Bake bread about 1 hour 20 minutes. Stand bread in pan 10 minutes; turn, top-side up, onto a wire rack to cool.

You will need about four large overripe bananas for the amount of mashed banana required.

SERVING SUGGESTION
Serve bread toasted with butter.

COCONUT
Banana Bread

PANETTONE

PREP + COOK TIME *1 HOUR 30 MINUTES (+ STANDING)* **SERVES** *20*

1¼ cups (200g) mixed dried fruit

⅓ cup (80ml) marsala

4 teaspoons (14g) dried yeast

¾ cup (180ml) warm milk

1 teaspoon caster (superfine) sugar

2½ cups (375g) plain (all-purpose) flour

¼ cup (55g) caster (superfine) sugar, extra

1 teaspoon salt

125g (4 ounces) butter, chopped finely, softened

1 teaspoon vanilla extract

2 eggs

2 egg yolks

1 egg, beaten lightly, extra

1. Combine fruit and marsala in a small bowl; stand 30 minutes.

2. Whisk yeast, milk and sugar in a small bowl until yeast dissolves. Cover; stand in a warm place about 10 minutes or until frothy.

3. Sift flour, extra sugar and salt into a large bowl; stir in yeast mixture, butter, extract, eggs, egg yolks and undrained fruit mixture. Beat vigorously with a wooden spoon about 5 minutes. (Mixture will be soft like cake batter, but will become elastic and start to leave the side of bowl.) Cover bowl; stand in a warm place about 1 hour or until dough has doubled in size.

4. Grease a deep 20cm (8-inch) round cake pan; line base and side with baking paper, extending the paper 5cm (2 inches) above sides.

5. Beat dough again with a wooden spoon 5 minutes; spread mixture into pan. Cover; stand in a warm place about 1 hour or until doubled in size.

6. Preheat oven to 200°C/400°F.

7. Brush top of panettone with extra egg. Bake about 1 hour 10 minutes or until panettone sounds hollow when tapped with fingertips. Stand panettone in pan 5 minutes; turn, top-side up, onto a wire rack to cool.

You can make baby panettone by dividing the dough evenly into a lined 6-hole (¾-cup/180ml) texas muffin pan at step 4. Continue recipe as above, reducing baking time to about 30 minutes. Panettone will keep in an airtight container for up to five days. Freeze panettone for up to three months.

CARAMEL CHOC CHIP
Fruit and Nut Buns

PREP + COOK TIME *1 HOUR 20 MINUTES (+ STANDING)* MAKES *12*

2 teaspoons (7g) dried yeast

1¼ cups (310ml) warm milk

¼ cup (55g) firmly packed light brown sugar

1 cup (150g) plain (all-purpose) flour

100g (3 ounces) butter, chopped finely, softened

1 egg

2 cups (300g) plain (all-purpose) flour, extra

1 teaspoon salt

2 teaspoons mixed spice

½ cup (80g) sultanas

½ cup (95g) dark choc bits

½ cup (80g) chopped mixed nuts

1 egg yolk, beaten lightly

CARAMEL ICING

½ cup (80g) icing (confectioners') sugar

1 tablespoon light brown sugar

2 teaspoons boiling water, approximately

1 Whisk yeast, milk and 2 teaspoons of the sugar in a large bowl until yeast dissolves; whisk in flour. Cover; stand in a warm place about 30 minutes or until frothy.

2 Stir butter, egg, remaining sugar and sifted extra flour, salt and spice into yeast mixture. Stir in sultanas, choc bits and nuts. Knead dough on a floured surface about 5 minutes or until smooth and elastic. Place dough in an oiled large bowl, cover; stand in a warm place about 1½ hours or until dough has doubled in size.

3 Punch down dough; knead on a floured surface until smooth. Divide dough into 12 portions; shape each portion into 15cm (6-inch) long buns. Place on an oiled oven tray, cover; stand in a warm place about 30 minutes or until doubled in size.

4 Preheat oven to 200°C/400°F.

5 Brush buns with egg yolk. Bake about 30 minutes or until buns sound hollow when tapped. Stand buns on tray 5 minutes; transfer to a wire rack to cool.

6 Meanwhile, make caramel icing.

7 Drizzle icing onto cooled buns; stand until icing is set.

CARAMEL ICING

Sift icing sugar into a small bowl; stir in brown sugar and the water until smooth and spreadable.

These buns are best made on the day of serving. Uniced buns can be frozen for three months.

FRUIT AND NUT
Loaf

PREP + COOK TIME *1 HOUR 20 MINUTES* *(+ STANDING)* **MAKES** *18 SLICES*

2 teaspoons (7g) dried yeast

¼ cup (55g) caster (superfine) sugar

2 tablespoons warm water

⅔ cup (160ml) warm milk

1 cup (150g) plain (all-purpose) flour

1 egg, beaten lightly

2 teaspoons finely grated orange rind

2 cups (300g) plain (all-purpose) flour, extra

1 teaspoon salt

½ teaspoon ground cinnamon

100g (3 ounces) butter, softened

¼ cup (40g) sultanas

¼ cup (35g) raisins

¼ cup (40g) dried currants

¼ cup (25g) coarsely chopped roasted walnuts

1 egg yolk

1 tablespoon caster (superfine) sugar, extra

½ teaspoon ground cinnamon, extra

1 Whisk yeast, 2 teaspoons of the sugar and the water in a large bowl until yeast dissolves. Whisk in milk and sifted flour, cover; stand in a warm place about 30 minutes or until mixture is frothy.

2 Stir in egg and rind, then sifted extra flour, salt, cinnamon and remaining sugar. Stir in butter, fruit and nuts.

3 Knead dough on a floured surface until smooth. Place dough in a large greased bowl, cover; stand in a warm place about 1½ hours or until dough has doubled in size.

4 Grease a 14cm x 21cm (5½-inch x 8½-inch) loaf pan; line base with baking paper.

5 Knead dough on a floured surface until smooth. Place into pan, cover loosely with greased plastic wrap; stand in a warm place about 30 minutes or until risen slightly.

6 Preheat oven to 200°C/400°F.

7 Remove plastic wrap. Brush dough with egg yolk; sprinkle dough with combined extra sugar and extra cinnamon.

8 Bake loaf 10 minutes. Reduce oven to 180°C/350°F; bake about 30 minutes or until loaf sounds hollow when tapped. Turn onto a wire rack to cool.

Be careful to measure all the ingredients exactly, too much or too little of some of the ingredients will affect the way the loaf rises.
This loaf can be frozen for up to three months.

CHAPTER 7

TINY &
TEMPTING

GLAZED ROSEWATER
Madeleines

PREP + COOK TIME *35 MINUTES (+ COOLING)* **MAKES** *24*

125g (4 ounces) butter, melted
1 tablespoon plain (all-purpose) flour
2 eggs
⅓ cup (75g) caster (superfine) sugar
2 teaspoons rosewater
1 teaspoon vanilla bean paste
⅔ cup (100g) plain (all-purpose) flour, extra
¼ teaspoon baking powder

GLACÉ ICING
1 cup (160g) icing (confectioners') sugar
1 teaspoon butter
2 tablespoons lemon juice, approximately
pink food colouring

1 Preheat oven to 200°C/400°F. Brush two 12-hole (1½-tablespoon/30ml) madeleine pans with 1 tablespoon of the melted butter. Dust with the flour; shake out excess.
2 Beat eggs, sugar, rosewater and paste in a small bowl with an electric mixer for about 5 minutes or until thick and creamy.
3 Meanwhile, sift extra flour and baking powder twice onto a piece of baking paper. Sift flour mixture over egg mixture; fold into egg mixture with remaining melted butter. Drop tablespoons of mixture into pan holes.
4 Bake madeleines about 10 minutes. Stand in pans 2 minutes; turn onto a wire rack to cool.
5 Meanwhile, make glacé icing.
6 Dip one end of each madeleine into icing; place on a baking-paper-covered wire rack 5 minutes or until set.

GLACÉ ICING

Sift icing sugar into a small heatproof bowl; stir
in butter and enough juice to make a thick paste.
Place the bowl over a small saucepan of simmering
water; stir until icing is of a pouring consistency
(do not overheat). Tint pink with colouring.

These madeleines are best made and eaten on
the same day.

ORANGE AND WHITE CHOCOLATE
Petit Fours

PREP + COOK TIME *55 MINUTES (+ STANDING)* **MAKES** *28*

180g (5½ ounces) butter, softened
¾ cup (165g) caster (superfine) sugar
3 teaspoons finely grated orange rind
3 eggs
½ cup (125ml) orange juice
1½ cups (225g) self-raising flour
2 tablespoons plain (all-purpose) flour
½ cup (125ml) pouring cream
180g (5½ ounces) white eating chocolate,
   chopped finely
2 x 5cm (2-inch) strips orange rind
½ cup (125ml) boiling water

1 Preheat oven to 180°C/350°F. Grease a 20cm x 30cm (8-inch x 12-inch) rectangular pan; line base and sides with baking paper, extending the paper 5cm (2 inches) over sides.

2 Beat butter, sugar and grated rind in a small bowl with electric mixer until light and fluffy. Beat in eggs, one at a time. Stir in juice and sifted flours. Spread mixture into pan.

3 Bake cake about 35 minutes. Stand in pan 10 minutes; transfer to a wire rack to cool. Using a 3.5cm (1½-inch) cutter, cut 28 rounds from cooled cake. Discard excess cake.

4 Bring cream to the boil in a small saucepan. Remove from heat; pour over chocolate in a small bowl, stir until smooth. Stand about 20 minutes or until thickened.

5 Slice strips of rind thinly; place in a small bowl with the boiling water. Soak 30 seconds; drain. Transfer rind to a small bowl of iced water; drain.

6 Place cake rounds on a wire rack over a baking-paper-lined tray; spread ganache on cakes, top with rind. Stand until set.

You can serve petit fours in patty paper cases.
You could use candied orange peel instead of the thinly sliced orange rind.
Petit fours are best made on the day of serving.

RASPBERRY ALMOND
Petit Fours

PREP + COOK TIME *55 MINUTES (+ STANDING)* **MAKES** *32*

125g (4 ounces) butter, softened
¾ cup (165g) caster (superfine) sugar
3 eggs
½ cup (75g) plain (all-purpose) flour
¼ cup (35g) self-raising flour
½ cup (60g) ground almonds
⅓ cup (80g) sour cream
150g (4½ ounces) fresh raspberries
32 ready-made icing flowers

ICING

2½ cups (400g) icing (confectioners') sugar
2 tablespoons lemon juice
1½ tablespoons boiling water, approximately

1 Preheat oven to 180°C/350°F. Grease a 20cm x 30cm (8-inch x 12-inch) rectangular pan; line base and sides with baking paper, extending the paper 5cm (2 inches) over sides.

2 Beat butter and sugar in a small bowl with an electric mixer until light and fluffy. Beat in eggs, one at a time. Stir in sifted flours, ground almonds, sour cream and raspberries. Spread mixture into pan.

3 Bake cake about 40 minutes. Stand in pan 10 minutes; transfer to a wire rack to cool. Using a serrated knife, trim and discard edges of cooled cake. Cut cake into 32 squares.

4 Make icing.

5 Place cake squares on a wire rack over a baking-paper-lined tray; spread or drizzle icing over squares. Top with icing flowers; stand until set.

ICING

Stir ingredients in a medium bowl to a smooth paste (add a little extra water for a thinner consistency if you like).

You can serve petit fours in patty paper cases.
You could top the petit fours with fresh raspberries instead of the icing flowers.
Petit fours are best made on the day of serving.

BLACK FOREST
Cupcakes

425g (13½ ounces) canned pitted cherries
   in syrup
155g (5 ounces) butter, chopped coarsely
100g (3½ ounces) dark eating (semi-sweet)
   chocolate, chopped coarsely
1⅓ cups (295g) caster (superfine) sugar
¼ cup (60ml) cherry brandy
1 cup (150g) plain (all-purpose) flour
2 tablespoons self-raising flour
2 tablespoons cocoa powder
1 egg
100g (3½ ounces) dark eating (semi-sweet)
   chocolate

CHERRY BRANDY CREAM

⅔ cup (160ml) thickened (heavy) cream
2 teaspoons cherry brandy

1. Preheat oven to 170°C/340°F. Line a 12-hole (⅓-cup/80ml) muffin pan with paper cases.
2. Drain cherries; reserve syrup. Process ½ cup cherries with ½ cup of the syrup until smooth. Halve remaining cherries; reserve for decorating cakes. Discard remaining syrup.
3. Stir butter, chocolate, sugar, brandy and cherry puree in a small saucepan, over low heat, until chocolate is melted. Transfer mixture to a medium bowl; cool 15 minutes.
4. Whisk sifted flours and cocoa, then egg into chocolate mixture. Spoon mixture into paper cases; smooth surface.
5. Bake cakes about 45 minutes. Stand in pan 5 minutes; turn, top-side up, onto a wire rack to cool.
6. Make cherry brandy cream.
7. Place remaining cherry halves on cakes, spoon cherry brandy cream on top. Using a vegetable peeler, grate chocolate; sprinkle over cream.

CHERRY BRANDY CREAM
Beat cream in a medium bowl with an electric mixer until firm peaks form. Stir in cherry brandy.

These cupcakes are best made on the day of serving. Plain cakes can be frozen for up to three months.

MINI DATE ORANGE
and Ginger Rock Cakes

MINI DATE ORANGE
and Ginger Rock Cakes

PREP + COOK TIME *35 MINUTES* **MAKES** *30*

2 cups (300g) self-raising flour
1 teaspoon ground ginger
⅓ cup (75g) caster (superfine) sugar
90g (3 ounces) butter, chopped coarsely
1 cup (140g) coarsely chopped dried dates
¼ cup (45g) finely chopped glacé ginger
2 teaspoons finely grated orange rind
1 egg, beaten lightly
½ cup (125ml) milk
1 tablespoon caster (superfine) sugar, extra

1 Preheat oven to 180°C/350°F. Grease oven trays.
2 Sift flour, ground ginger and sugar into a large bowl; rub in butter. Stir in dates, glacé ginger and rind, then combined egg and milk (do not overmix).
3 Drop level tablespoons of mixture, about 5cm (2 inches) apart, onto trays; sprinkle with extra sugar.
4 Bake rock cakes about 15 minutes. Cool on trays.

These rock cakes are best made and eaten on the same day.

SERVING SUGGESTION
Serve warm rock cakes with butter.

CHOCOLATE LIQUEUR TRUFFLE
Squares

PREP + COOK TIME *20 MINUTES (+ REFRIGERATION)* **MAKES** *96*

185g (6 ounces) milk eating chocolate, chopped coarsely
2 teaspoons vegetable oil
¾ cup (180ml) thickened (heavy) cream
500g (1 pound) dark eating (semi-sweet) chocolate, chopped finely
¼ cup (60ml) hazelnut-flavoured liqueur
1 cup (140g) roasted hazelnuts, chopped finely

1 Grease a 20cm x 30cm (8-inch x 12-inch) rectangular pan; line base and long sides with baking paper, extending the paper 5cm (2 inches) over sides.
2 Stir milk chocolate and oil in a small heatproof bowl over a small saucepan of simmering water until smooth. Spread mixture over base of pan. Freeze 5 minutes.
3 Meanwhile, bring cream to the boil in a medium saucepan. Remove from heat; add dark chocolate, stir until smooth. Stir in liqueur.
4 Spread dark chocolate mixture over milk chocolate in pan; sprinkle with nuts. Refrigerate 3 hours or overnight before cutting.

These squares will keep in an airtight container in the fridge for up to a week.

(PHOTOGRAPH PAGE 258)

CHOCOLATE LIQUEUR
Truffle Squares
(RECIPE PAGE 257)

WHITE CHOCOLATE, PASSIONFRUIT
and Coconut Crunch Truffles

(RECIPE PAGE 260)

WHITE CHOCOLATE, PASSIONFRUIT
and Coconut Crunch Truffles

PREP + COOK TIME *45 MINUTES (+ REFRIGERATION)* **MAKES** *24*

450g (14 ounces) white eating chocolate
250g (8 ounces) butternut snap biscuits
½ cup (40g) desiccated coconut
½ cup (125ml) passionfruit pulp
2 cups (160g) toasted shredded coconut

1. Place 180g (5½ ounces) of the chocolate in a small heatproof bowl over a small saucepan of simmering water; stir until melted.
2. Process biscuits until fine; transfer to a medium bowl. Stir in desiccated coconut, passionfruit and melted chocolate. Cover; refrigerate 1 hour or until firm.
3. Roll level tablespoons of mixture into balls. Place on a baking-paper-lined oven tray; refrigerate 1 hour or until firm.
4. Place remaining chocolate in a small heatproof bowl over a small saucepan of simmering water; stir until melted.
5. Place shredded coconut in a small shallow bowl. Dip balls in melted chocolate using two forks; drain off excess. Roll in shredded coconut. Return to tray; refrigerate 30 minutes or until set.

These truffles will keep in an airtight container in the fridge for up to a week

(PHOTOGRAPH PAGE 259)

WICKED CHOC
Nut Bites

PREP + COOK TIME *45 MINUTES (+ REFRIGERATION)* **MAKES** *30*

4 sheets confectioners' rice paper
375g (12 ounces) dark choc Melts
⅓ cup (80ml) milk
20g (¾ ounce) butter
⅓ cup (95g) crunchy peanut butter
375g (12 ounces) white marshmallows
1 cup (140g) salted peanuts

1. Grease a deep 20cm (8-inch) square cake pan; line base with rice paper, trimming to fit.
2. Stir choc Melts, milk, butter, peanut butter and marshmallows in a large heatproof bowl over a large saucepan of simmering water until smooth. Remove from heat; stir in nuts.
3. Spread mixture into pan; cover with remaining rice paper, trimming to fit. Refrigerate 1 hour or until firm.
4. Place a slightly smaller cake pan on top of nougat; weight with cans. Refrigerate overnight until firm before cutting into squares.

Confectioners' rice paper is edible and ready to use. It can be bought from specialty food stores. Don't confuse this rice paper with the one used in recipes such as fresh rice paper rolls, which needs soaking to soften.
These bites will keep in an airtight container in the fridge for up to a week

WICKED CHOC
Nut Bites

FROU FROU CAKES

PREP + COOK TIME *1 HOUR* MAKES *12*

125g (4 ounces) butter, softened
1 cup (220g) caster (superfine) sugar
3 eggs
½ cup (75g) plain (all-purpose) flour
¼ cup (35g) self-raising flour
½ cup (40g) desiccated coconut
⅓ cup (80g) sour cream
155g (5 ounces) frozen raspberries (see notes)
1 cup (50g) flaked coconut, toasted
15 fresh raspberries, halved

CREAM CHEESE FROSTING

60g (2 ounces) butter, softened
155g (5 ounces) cream cheese, softened
2 teaspoons coconut extract
3 cups (480g) icing (confectioners') sugar

1 Preheat oven to 180°C/350°F. Line a 12-hole (⅓-cup/80ml) muffin pan with paper cases.

2 Beat butter, sugar and eggs in a small bowl with an electric mixer until light and fluffy. Stir in sifted flours, desiccated coconut, sour cream and frozen raspberries. Spoon mixture into paper cases; smooth surface.

3 Bake cakes about 40 minutes. Stand in pan 5 minutes; turn, top-side up, onto a wire rack to cool. Remove paper cases from cold cakes.

4 Make cream cheese frosting.

5 Spread top and side of cakes with frosting; decorate with flaked coconut and fresh raspberries.

CREAM CHEESE FROSTING

Beat butter, cream cheese and extract in a small bowl with an electric mixer until light and fluffy; gradually beat in sifted icing sugar.

Do not thaw the frozen raspberries as their colour will bleed into the cake.
These cakes are best made on the day of serving. Unfrosted cakes can be frozen for up to three months.

PASSIONFRUIT CURD
and Coconut Tarts

PREP + COOK TIME *1 HOUR 15 MINUTES (+ COOLING & REFRIGERATION)* MAKES *12*

1 cup (80g) desiccated coconut
1 egg white, beaten lightly
2 tablespoons caster (superfine) sugar
¼ cup (60ml) thickened (heavy) cream
1 tablespoon passionfruit pulp

PASSIONFRUIT CURD
½ cup (125ml) passionfruit pulp
½ teaspoon finely grated lemon rind
1 tablespoon lemon juice
½ cup (110g) caster (superfine) sugar
80g (2½ ounces) butter, chopped coarsely
1 egg, beaten lightly
1 egg yolk

1 Make passionfruit curd.
2 Preheat oven to 150°C/300°F. Grease a 12-hole (1-tablespoon/20ml) mini muffin pan.
3 Combine coconut, egg white and sugar in a small bowl. Press mixture firmly and evenly over bases and sides of pan holes.
4 Bake tart cases about 20 minutes or until browned lightly around the edges. Cool in pan.
5 Meanwhile, beat cream in a small bowl with an electric mixer until firm peaks form; fold into ½ cup of the passionfruit curd. Reserve remaining curd for another use.
6 Transfer coconut cases to a serving plate; spoon passionfruit curd mixture into cases. Top each tart with a little passionfruit pulp.

PASSIONFRUIT CURD
Press passionfruit pulp firmly through a sieve over a small bowl. You will need ¼ cup passionfruit juice for this recipe. Discard seeds. Combine passionfruit juice with remaining ingredients in a medium heatproof bowl; stir over a medium saucepan of simmering water about 10 minutes or until mixture thickly coats the back of a wooden spoon. Cool; refrigerate 2 hours or until cold.

You will need about six passionfruit for this recipe. Remaining passionfruit curd is delicious spread on scones or used as a filling for pavlovas.
These tarts are best made on the day of serving.

BRANDY SNAP BASKETS
with Hazelnut Cream

PREP + COOK TIME *1 HOUR* MAKES *45*

1 tablespoon golden syrup or treacle
30g (1 ounce) butter
1½ tablespoons light brown sugar
1½ tablespoons plain (all-purpose) flour
1 teaspoon ground ginger
45 (⅓ cup) roasted hazelnuts, skins removed

HAZELNUT CREAM
¾ cup (180ml) thickened (heavy) cream
1 tablespoon hazelnut-flavoured liqueur

1 Preheat oven to 180°C/350°F. Grease two oven trays.
2 Stir syrup, butter and sugar in a small saucepan over low heat until smooth. Remove pan from heat; stir in sifted flour and ginger.
3 Drop four level ¼-teaspoons of mixture, about 5cm (2 inches) apart, on oven trays (for easier handling, bake only four at a time).
4 Bake about 4 minutes or until golden brown. Remove from oven; cool on tray 30 seconds. With a rounded knife or metal spatula, quickly lift brandy snap from tray; shape each brandy snap into a basket-shape using an upturned foil petit-four case as a guide. Repeat with remaining mixture.
5 Make hazelnut cream.
6 Just before serving, fill baskets with hazelnut cream; top each with a nut.

HAZELNUT CREAM
Beat cream and liqueur in a small bowl with an electric mixer until firm peaks form.

This recipe makes a lot of tiny baskets; make as many as you need, then make the remaining mixture into larger snaps – serve them stacked, layered with cream for an easy dessert.

HONEY GINGER
Crunchies

PREP + COOK TIME *25 MINUTES* **MAKES** *24*

25g (¾ ounce) butter
1 tablespoon honey
1½ cups (60g) cornflakes
¼ cup (20g) flaked almonds, roasted
¼ cup (55g) finely chopped glacé ginger

1 Preheat oven to 180°C/350°F. Line two 12-hole (1-tablespoon/20ml) mini muffin pans with foil cases.
2 Melt butter and honey in a small saucepan. Combine butter mixture with cornflakes, nuts and ginger in a large bowl.
3 Spoon level tablespoons of cornflake mixture into foil cases.
4 Bake crunchies about 10 minutes or until golden. Cool in pans.

These crunchies can be made a week ahead. Keep in an airtight container in the fridge.

COCONUT ICE

PREP TIME *15 MINUTES (+ REFRIGERATION)* **MAKES** *64*

5¼ cups (840g) icing (confectioners') sugar
2½ cups (200g) desiccated coconut
395g (12½ ounces) canned sweetened
    condensed milk
1 egg white, beaten lightly
pink food colouring

1 Line a deep 20cm (8-inch) square cake pan with strips of baking paper.
2 Sift icing sugar into a large bowl; stir in coconut, then condensed milk and egg white.
3 Divide mixture in half; tint half pink with colouring. Press pink mixture into pan, then top with white mixture. Cover; refrigerate about 3 hours or until set before cutting into small squares.

Coconut ice will keep in an aitright container in the fridge for up to two weeks.

HONEY GINGER
Crunchies

COCONUT ICE

BUTTERFLY CAKES

(RECIPE PAGE 275)

BUTTERFLY CAKES

PREP + COOK TIME *50 MINUTES* **MAKES** *24*

125g (4 ounces) butter, softened
⅔ cup (150g) caster (superfine) sugar
3 eggs
1 teaspoon vanilla extract
1½ cups (225g) self-raising flour
¼ cup (60ml) milk
1¼ cups (310ml) thickened (heavy) cream
   (see notes)
½ cup (160g) jam
1 tablespoon icing (confectioners') sugar

1 Preheat oven to 180°C/350°F. Line two 12-hole (2-tablespoon/40ml) deep flat-based patty pans with paper cases.

2 Beat butter, caster sugar, eggs, extract, sifted flour and milk in a small bowl with an electric mixer on low speed until ingredients are just combined. Increase speed to medium; beat about 3 minutes or until mixture is smooth and pale in colour. Drop slightly rounded tablespoons of mixture into paper cases.

3 Bake cakes about 20 minutes. Stand cakes in pans 5 minutes; turn, top-sides up, onto wire racks to cool.

4 Beat cream in a small bowl with an electric mixer until firm peaks form.

5 Using a sharp pointed vegetable knife, cut a circle from the top of each cake; cut circle in half to make two "wings". Fill cavities with jam and whipped cream; position wings on top of cakes, dust with sifted icing sugar.

You can use just one 300ml carton of cream for this recipe.
Use whatever jam you like or some thick pureed fruit. Lemon butter is another popular filling.
Decorate and fill cakes up to an hour before serving.
Plain cakes can be frozen for up to three months.

WHITE CHOC-CHIP, ORANGE AND
Cranberry Mini Muffins

PREP + COOK TIME *40 MINUTES* MAKES *48*

2 cups (300g) self-raising flour
½ cup (110g) caster (superfine) sugar
¾ cup (135g) white choc bits
½ cup (65g) dried cranberries
60g (2 ounces) butter, melted
¾ cup (180ml) milk
1 egg, beaten lightly
2 teaspoons finely grated orange rind
¼ cup (60ml) orange juice

GLACÉ ICING
1½ cups (240g) icing (confectioners') sugar
½ teaspoon vegetable oil
2 tablespoons water, approximately
pink, blue, green and yellow food colouring

1 Preheat oven to 200°C/400°F. Line four 12-hole (1-tablespoon/20ml) mini muffin pans with paper cases.
2 Sift flour and sugar into a medium bowl; stir in remaining ingredients. Spoon mixture into paper cases.
3 Bake muffins about 10 minutes. Stand in pans 2 minutes; turn, top-side up, onto wire racks to cool.
4 Meanwhile, make glacé icing.
5 Spread icing on cold muffins.

GLACÉ ICING
Sift icing sugar into a small heatproof bowl. Stir in oil and enough water to make a paste. Stir over a small saucepan of simmering water until icing is spreadable. Divide icing evenly into four small bowls; tint each icing with one of the four food colourings.

These muffins are best made on the day of serving. Plain muffins can be frozen for up to three months.

CHOC-ORANGE TRUFFLES
with Boozy Prunes and Ginger

PREP + COOK TIME *1 HOUR (+ STANDING & REFRIGERATION)* **MAKES 24**

450g (14½ ounces) dark eating (semi-sweet)
   chocolate, chopped coarsely
½ cup (125ml) thickened (heavy) cream
½ cup (50g) cocoa powder

BOOZY PRUNES AND GINGER
⅓ cup (60g) finely chopped prunes
2 tablespoons finely chopped glacé ginger
2 teaspoons finely grated orange rind
1 tablespoon orange-flavoured liqueur

1 Make boozy prunes and ginger.
2 Place chocolate and cream in a medium heatproof
   bowl over a medium saucepan of simmering water;
   stir until smooth. Stand at room temperature until
   mixture starts to thicken. Stir in prune mixture.
   Refrigerate about 2 hours or until firm.
3 Sift cocoa into a medium bowl. Roll level tablespoons
   of chocolate mixture into balls; roll in cocoa.
   Place on a tray; refrigerate until firm.
4 Remove from refrigerator 30 minutes before serving.
   Dust with a little extra sifted cocoa.

BOOZY PRUNES AND GINGER
Combine ingredients in a small bowl. Cover;
stand overnight.

Grand Marnier or Cointreau can be used for the
orange-flavoured liqueur.
These truffles can be stored in an airtight container
in the fridge for up to three weeks. Truffles, without
their cocoa powder coating, can be frozen for up
to three months. Remove from the freezer an hour
before rolling in cocoa powder. Dust with extra
sifted cocoa just before serving.

WHITE CHOCOLATE
Lamingtons

PREP + COOK TIME *1 HOUR (+ REFRIGERATION & STANDING)* MAKES *35*

6 eggs

⅔ cup (150g) caster (superfine) sugar

80g (2½ ounces) white eating chocolate, chopped finely

½ cup (75g) plain (all-purpose) flour

⅓ cup (50g) self-raising flour

⅓ cup (50g) cornflour (cornstarch)

2 cups (150g) desiccated coconut

100g (3 ounces) white eating chocolate, grated finely

ICING

4 cups (640g) icing (confectioners') sugar

¾ cup (180ml) milk

1 Preheat oven to 180°C/350°F. Grease a 20cm x 30cm (8-inch x 12-inch) rectangular pan; line base and sides with baking paper, extending the paper 5cm (2 inches) over sides.

2 Beat eggs in a medium bowl with an electric mixer about 10 minutes or until thick and creamy. Gradually add sugar, beating until sugar dissolves. Fold in chopped chocolate and triple-sifted flours. Spread mixture into pan.

3 Bake cake about 35 minutes. Turn cake onto a baking-paper-covered wire rack to cool; refrigerate until required.

4 Make icing.

5 Cut cold cake into 35 squares; dip each square in icing, drain off excess. Toss squares in combined coconut and grated chocolate; place on a wire rack to set.

ICING

Sift icing sugar into a medium heatproof bowl; stir in milk. Place over a medium saucepan of simmering water; stir until icing is of a coating consistency.

Lamingtons can be made one day ahead of serving. Keep them in an airtight container in the fridge. The un-cut cake can be frozen for up to three months.

MINI LIME AND BERRY
Friands

MINI LIME AND BERRY
Friands

PREP + COOK TIME *25 MINUTES* **MAKES** *24*

3 egg whites
90g (3 ounces) unsalted butter, melted
1 teaspoon finely grated lime rind
½ cup (60g) ground almonds
¾ cup (120g) icing (confectioners') sugar
¼ cup (35g) plain (all-purpose) flour
⅓ cup (50g) frozen blueberries
1 tablespoon icing (confectioners') sugar, extra

1. Preheat oven to 180°C/350°F. Grease two 12-hole (1-tablespoon/20ml) mini muffin pans.
2. Whisk egg whites in a medium bowl with a fork until frothy. Stir in butter, rind, ground almonds and sifted icing sugar and flour.
3. Spoon heaped teaspoons of mixture into each pan hole; top each with a blueberry.
4. Bake friands about 10 minutes. Stand in pans 5 minutes; turn onto a wire rack to cool. Dust with sifted extra icing sugar.

These friands will keep in an airtight container for up to three days. They can be frozen for up to three months.

FIG AND WALNUT
Friand Slice

PREP + COOK TIME *40 MINUTES* **MAKES** *20*

1¼ cups (125g) roasted walnuts
6 egg whites
185g (6 ounces) unsalted butter, melted
1½ cups (240g) icing (confectioners') sugar
½ cup (75g) plain (all-purpose) flour
2 teaspoons finely grated orange rind
1 tablespoon orange juice
4 dried figs (85g), sliced thinly
1 tablespoon icing (confectioners') sugar, extra

1. Preheat oven to 200°C/400°F. Grease a 20cm x 30cm (8-inch x 12-inch) rectangular pan; line base and sides with baking paper, extending the paper 5cm (2 inches) over sides.
2. Process nuts until ground finely.
3. Whisk egg whites in a medium bowl with a fork until frothy. Stir in butter, sifted icing sugar and flour, rind, juice and ground nuts. Spread mixture in pan; top with slices of fig.
4. Bake slice about 25 minutes or until golden. Cool in pan. Dust with sifted extra icing sugar before cutting into pieces.

This slice will keep in an airtight container for up to three days. It can be frozen for up to three months.

(PHOTOGRAPH PAGE 284)

FIG AND WALNUT
Friand Slice

(RECIPE PAGE 283)

MINI CHOC-CHIP
Friands
(RECIPE PAGE 286)

MINI CHOC-CHIP
Friands

PREP + COOK TIME *40 MINUTES (+ STANDING)* **MAKES** *18*

3 egg whites
90g (3 ounces) butter, melted
½ cup (60g) ground almonds
¾ cup (120g) icing (confectioners') sugar
¼ cup (35g) plain (all-purpose) flour
100g (3 ounces) dark eating (semi-sweet)
    chocolate, chopped finely
¼ cup (60ml) pouring cream
100g (3 ounces) dark eating (semi-sweet)
    chocolate, chopped coarsely, extra

1　Preheat oven to 180°C/350°F. Grease 18 holes of
   two 12-hole (1-tablespoon/20ml) mini muffin pans.
2　Whisk egg whites in medium bowl with a fork.
   Stir in butter, ground almonds, sifted icing sugar
   and flour until combined. Stir in chopped
   chocolate. Spoon mixture into pan holes.
3　Bake friands about 15 minutes. Turn, top-side up,
   onto wire racks to cool.
4　Place cream and extra chocolate in a medium
   heatproof bowl over a medium saucepan of
   simmering water; stir until smooth. Stand until
   thickened. Spread chocolate mixture on top
   of friands.

These friands will keep in an airtight container in
the fridge for up to three days. Uniced friands can
be frozen for up to three months.

(PHOTOGRAPH PAGE 285)

MINI BAKED LEMON
Cheesecakes

PREP + COOK TIME *50 MINUTES (+ REFRIGERATION)* **MAKES** *12*

100g (3½ ounces) plain sweet biscuits
45g (1½ ounces) butter, melted
500g (1 pound) cream cheese, softened
2 teaspoons finely grated lemon rind
½ cup (110g) caster (superfine) sugar
2 eggs
APRICOT BRANDY GLAZE
⅔ cup (220g) apricot jam
2 tablespoons brandy

1　Preheat oven to 150°C/300°F. Line a 12-hole
   (⅓-cup/80ml) muffin pan with paper cases.
2　Blend or process biscuits until fine. Add butter;
   process until just combined. Divide mixture
   into paper cases; press down firmly. Refrigerate
   30 minutes.
3　Beat cream cheese, rind and sugar in a small bowl
   with an electric mixer until smooth. Beat in eggs.
   Pour mixture into paper cases.
4　Bake cheesecakes about 25 minutes. Stand in
   pan 5 minutes; turn, top-side up, onto a wire rack
   to cool.
5　Make apricot brandy glaze. Pour glaze evenly
   over cheesecake tops; refrigerate 2 hours or until
   glaze is set.

APRICOT BRANDY GLAZE
Heat ingredients in a small saucepan over low heat;
strain.

These cheesecakes are best eaten within two days
of making them. Keep them in an airtight container
in the fridge.

MINI BAKED LEMON
Cheesecakes

ANGEL CAKES

PREP + COOK TIME *1 HOUR (+ STANDING)* MAKES *12*

90g (3 ounces) butter, softened
½ cup (110g) caster (superfine) sugar
2 eggs
½ teaspoon vanilla extract
1 cup (150g) self-raising flour
2 tablespoons milk
1 cup (80g) desiccated coconut
½ cup (125ml) thickened (heavy) cream
¼ cup (100g) raspberry jam

CHOCOLATE ICING

15g (½ ounce) butter
⅓ cup (80ml) milk
2 cups (320g) icing (confectioners') sugar
¼ cup (25g) cocoa powder

1 Preheat oven to 180°C/350°F. Line a 12-hole (⅓-cup/80ml) muffin pan with paper cases.
2 Beat butter, sugar, eggs, extract, sifted flour and milk in a small bowl with an electric mixer on low speed until ingredients are just combined. Increase speed to medium; beat until mixture has changed to a paler colour. Spoon mixture into paper cases; smooth surface.
3 Bake cakes 20 minutes. Stand in pan 5 minutes; turn, top-side up, onto a wire rack to cool. Remove paper cases from cold cakes.
4 Make chocolate icing.
5 Dip cakes in icing; drain off excess, toss cakes in coconut. Stand cakes on wire rack until set.
6 Meanwhile, beat cream in a small bowl until firm peaks form.
7 Cut cakes as desired; fill with jam and cream.

CHOCOLATE ICING
Melt butter in a medium heatproof bowl over a medium saucepan of simmering water. Stir in milk and sifted icing sugar and cocoa until icing is of a coating consistency.

These cakes will keep in an airtight container in the fridge for up to two days. Plain cakes can be frozen for up to three months.

MINI CHOCOLATE
Heart Cupcakes

PREP + COOK TIME *1 HOUR* MAKES *18*

30g (1 ounce) dark eating (semi-sweet) chocolate, chopped coarsely

⅓ cup (80ml) water

45g (1½ ounces) butter, softened

½ cup (110g) firmly packed light brown sugar

1 egg

⅓ cup (50g) self-raising flour

1 tablespoon cocoa powder

2 tablespoons ground almonds

100g (3 ounces) white chocolate Melts

BUTTERCREAM

90g (3 ounces) butter, softened

1 cup (240g) icing (confectioners') sugar

1 tablespoon milk

pink and blue food colouring

1 Preheat oven to 170°C/340°F. Line 18 holes of two 12-hole (1-tablespoon/20ml) mini muffin pans with paper cases.

2 Stir chocolate and the water in a small saucepan over low heat until smooth.

3 Beat butter, sugar and egg in a small bowl with an electric mixer until light and fluffy. Stir in sifted flour and cocoa, ground almonds and warm chocolate mixture. Drop level tablespoons of mixture into each paper case.

4 Bake cakes about 15 minutes. Stand in pans 5 minutes; turn, top-side up, onto wire racks to cool.

5 Meanwhile, stir chocolate Melts in a small heatproof bowl over a small saucepan of simmering water until melted. Spread a thin layer of chocolate on a sheet of baking paper; stand at room temperature until set. Using a 2cm (¾-inch) heart-shaped cutter, cut 18 hearts from chocolate.

6 Make buttercream.

7 Spread tops of cold cakes with generous spoonfuls of pink and blue buttercreams. Gently push hearts into buttercream.

BUTTERCREAM

Beat butter in a small bowl with an electric mixer until as white as possible; beat in sifted icing sugar and milk, in two batches. Divide into two small bowls; tint one pale pink and the other pale blue.

Decorate cakes up to three hours before serving. Plain cakes can be frozen for up to three months.

VERYBERRY CUPCAKES

PREP + COOK TIME *1 HOUR (+ STANDING)* **MAKES** *12*

125g (4 ounces) butter, softened
⅔ cup (150g) caster (superfine) sugar
½ teaspoon vanilla extract
2 eggs
1 cup (150g) dried mixed berries
½ cup (70g) slivered almonds
⅔ cup (100g) plain (all-purpose) flour
⅓ cup (50g) self-raising flour
¼ cup (60ml) milk

SUGARED FRUIT

1 egg white
155g (5 ounces) fresh blueberries
125g (4 ounces) fresh raspberries
2 tablespoons vanilla sugar

CREAM CHEESE FROSTING

30g (1 ounce) butter, softened
90g (3 ounces) cream cheese, softened
1½ cups (240g) icing (confectioners') sugar

1 Make sugared fruit.
2 Preheat oven to 170°C/340°F. Line a 12-hole (⅓-cup/80ml) muffin pan with paper cases.
3 Beat butter, sugar, extract and eggs in a small bowl with an electric mixer until light and fluffy. Stir in fruit and nuts, then sifted flours and milk. Spoon mixture into paper cases; smooth surface.
4 Bake cakes about 35 minutes. Stand in pan 5 minutes; turn, top-side up, onto a wire rack to cool.
5 Make cream cheese frosting.
6 Spread cold cakes with frosting; decorate with sugared fruit.

SUGARED FRUIT

Brush a tiny amount of unbeaten egg white all over each berry; roll fruit in vanilla sugar. Place fruit on a baking-paper-lined tray. Stand about 1 hour or until sugar is dry.

CREAM CHEESE FROSTING

Beat butter and cream cheese in a small bowl with an electric mixer until light and fluffy; gradually beat in sifted icing sugar.

Decorate cakes up to three hours before serving. Plain cakes can be frozen for up to three months.

BLUEBERRIES AND
Cream Cupcakes

PREP + COOK TIME *40 MINUTES* **MAKES** *8*

90g (3 ounces) butter, softened
½ cup (110g) caster (superfine) sugar
1 teaspoon finely grated lemon rind
2 eggs
1 cup (150g) self-raising flour
2 tablespoons milk
1 cup (250ml) thickened (heavy) cream
2 tablespoons icing (confectioners') sugar
315g (10 ounces) fresh blueberries

1 Preheat oven to 180°C/350°F. Line eight holes of a 12-hole (⅓-cup/80ml) muffin pan with paper cases.
2 Beat butter, caster sugar, rind, eggs, sifted flour and milk in a small bowl with an electric mixer on low speed until ingredients are combined. Increase speed to medium; beat until mixture has changed to a paler colour. Drop ¼ cup of mixture into each paper case.
3 Bake cakes about 20 minutes. Stand in pan 5 minutes; turn, top-side up, onto a wire rack to cool.
4 Beat cream and half the icing sugar in a small bowl with an electric mixer until soft peaks form.
5 Spread cold cakes with generous spoonfuls of cream; top with blueberries. Dust cakes with remaining sifted icing sugar.

Decorate cakes up to three hours before serving. Plain cakes can be frozen for up to three months.

SUGAR AND LACE
Caramel Cupcakes

PREP + COOK TIME *50 MINUTES (+ COOLING)* **MAKES** *12*

125g (4 ounces) butter, chopped coarsely
100g (3½ ounces) white eating chocolate, chopped coarsely
⅔ cup (150g) firmly packed light brown sugar
¼ cup (90g) golden syrup or treacle
⅔ cup (160ml) milk
1 cup (150g) plain (all-purpose) flour
⅓ cup (50g) self-raising flour
1 egg
½ cup (80g) icing (confectioners') sugar

1 Preheat oven to 170°C/340°F. Line a 12-hole (⅓-cup/80ml) muffin pan with paper cases.
2 Stir butter, chocolate, brown sugar, syrup and milk in a small saucepan, over low heat, until smooth. Transfer mixture to a medium bowl; cool 15 minutes.
3 Whisk sifted flours into chocolate mixture, then whisk in egg. Spoon mixture into paper cases.
4 Bake cakes about 30 minutes. Stand in pan 5 minutes; turn, top-side up, onto a wire rack to cool.
5 Just before serving, place a doily, lace or stencil over cold cake; sift a little icing sugar over doily, then carefully lift doily away from cake. Repeat with remaining cakes and icing sugar.

You will need some lace, a doily or a stencil for decorating these cakes.
Plain cakes can be frozen for up to three months.

BLUEBERRIES AND
Cream Cupcakes

SUGAR AND LACE
Caramel Cupcakes

CHAPTER 8

BIRTHDAYS & CHRISTMAS

LEMON CURD MERINGUE CAKE
with Toffee-dipped Blueberries

PREP + COOK TIME 1 HOUR 45 MINUTES (+ REFRIGERATION, COOLING & STANDING) SERVES 12

1 cup (150g) almond kernels
4 egg whites
1 cup (220g) caster (superfine) sugar
125g (4 ounces) white eating chocolate,
   grated coarsely
2½ cups (625ml) thick (double) cream (see note)

LEMON CURD

250g (8 ounces) cold butter, chopped coarsely
2 eggs, beaten lightly
⅔ cup (160ml) lemon juice
1⅓ cups (300g) caster (superfine) sugar
2 egg yolks

TOFFEE-DIPPED BLUEBERRIES

1 cup (220g) white (granulated) sugar
½ cup (125ml) water
125g (4 ounces) fresh blueberries

1 Make lemon curd.
2 Preheat oven to 160°C/325°F. Grease a 24cm
   (9½-inch) closed springform pan; insert base of
   pan upside down to make cake easier to remove.
   Line base with baking paper.
3 Spread nuts, in a single layer, on an oven tray; roast,
   uncovered, about 12 minutes or until skins begin
   to split. Cool. Chop nuts finely.
4 Beat egg whites and ¼ cup of the sugar in a small
   bowl with an electric mixer until firm peaks form.
   Add remaining sugar; beat on high speed about
   5 minutes or until sugar is dissolved. Fold in
   chocolate and nuts. Spread mixture into pan.
5 Bake meringue about 40 minutes. Cool in pan.

6 Beat half the cream in a small bowl with an
   electric mixer until soft peaks form; fold in curd.
   Spoon curd mixture onto meringue. Refrigerate
   several hours or overnight until firm.
7 Before serving, make toffee-dipped blueberries.
   Spoon remaining cream onto cake; top with
   toffee-dipped berries. Serve immediately.

LEMON CURD

Place butter in a medium saucepan; strain egg into
pan. Add remaining ingredients; stir over low heat,
without boiling, about 10 minutes or until mixture
thickly coats the back of a spoon. Transfer curd to a
medium heatproof bowl; refrigerate until cold.

TOFFEE-DIPPED BLUEBERRIES

Stir sugar and the water in a small saucepan over
medium heat until sugar is dissolved. Bring to the
boil; boil, without stirring, until sugar has thickened
and turns a caramel colour. Push a wooden
toothpick into each blueberry. Remove toffee from
heat; allow bubbles to subside. Working with one
blueberry at a time, holding by the toothpick, dip
berry into thickened toffee. Hold berry above toffee
so a trail of toffee falls from the berry. Hold upside
down until starting to set. You may need to reheat
the toffee if it starts to thicken too much.

You can use two 300ml cartons of cream for this
recipe; one for the curd mixture and one to spoon
onto the cake.

MIXED BERRY
Hazelnut Cake

PREP + COOK TIME *2 HOURS (+ REFRIGERATION)* **SERVES** *24*

250g (8 ounces) unsalted butter, softened
1½ cups (330g) caster (superfine) sugar
6 eggs
1 cup (150g) plain (all-purpose) flour
½ cup (75g) self-raising flour
1 cup (110g) ground hazelnuts
⅔ cup (160g) sour cream
300g (10 ounces) fresh mixed berries

WHITE CHOCOLATE GANACHE

¾ cup (180ml) thickened (heavy) cream
1 tablespoon blackcurrant-flavoured liqueur
375g (12 ounces) white eating chocolate,
 chopped coarsely

SUGARED BERRIES

125g (4 ounces) fresh raspberries
125g (4 ounces) fresh blueberries
1 egg white, beaten lightly
¼ cup (55g) caster (superfine) sugar

1 Make white chocolate ganache.
2 Preheat oven to 180°C/350°F. Grease a deep 23cm x 31cm (9-inch x 12 inch) oval cake pan; line base and side with baking paper.
3 Beat butter and sugar in a small bowl with an electric mixer until light and fluffy. Beat in eggs, one at a time. Transfer mixture to a large bowl; stir in sifted flours, ground hazelnuts, sour cream and berries. Spread mixture into pan.
4 Bake cake about 1½ hours. Stand in pan 10 minutes; turn, top-side up, onto a wire rack to cool.
5 Meanwhile, make sugared berries.
6 Spread cake with ganache; top with sugared berries. Serve immediately.

WHITE CHOCOLATE GANACHE

Bring cream and liqueur to the boil in a medium saucepan. Remove from heat; pour over chocolate in a small heatproof bowl, stir until smooth. Cover; refrigerate overnight. Beat ganache in a small bowl with an electric mixer until mixture changes to a paler colour.

SUGARED BERRIES

Using a small artist's paint brush, brush berries very lightly with egg white; toss in sugar. Place in a single layer on a tray; allow to dry at room temperature.

You can use frozen berries in the cake mixture, make sure to use them while they're still frozen. Plain cake can be frozen for up to three months.

HAZELNUT MUD CAKE
with Fudge Frosting

PREP + COOK TIME 2 HOURS (+ COOLING) SERVES 12

360g (11½ ounces) dark eating (semi-sweet) chocolate, chopped coarsely

225g (7 ounces) butter, chopped coarsely

¾ cup (165g) firmly packed light brown sugar

¾ cup (180ml) water

¾ cup (110g) plain (all-purpose) flour

¼ cup (35g) self-raising flour

½ cup (50g) ground hazelnuts

2 eggs

⅓ cup (80ml) hazelnut-flavoured liqueur

FUDGE FROSTING

45g (1½ ounces) butter, chopped coarsely

⅓ cup (75g) firmly packed light brown sugar

1 tablespoon water

2 tablespoons hazelnut-flavoured liqueur

1 cup (160g) icing (confectioners') sugar

2 tablespoons cocoa powder

1 Preheat oven to 150°C/300°F. Grease a deep 20cm (8-inch) round cake pan; line base and side with baking paper.

2 Stir chocolate, butter, sugar and the water in a medium saucepan over low heat until smooth. Transfer to a medium bowl; cool 15 minutes.

3 Stir sifted flours, ground hazelnuts, eggs and liqueur into chocolate mixture. Pour mixture into pan.

4 Bake cake about 1 hour 35 minutes. Stand in pan 5 minutes; turn, top-side up, onto a wire rack to cool.

5 Meanwhile, make fudge frosting.

6 Spread cake with frosting.

FUDGE FROSTING

Stir butter, brown sugar and the water in a small saucepan over heat, without boiling, until sugar dissolves. Remove from heat; stir in liqueur. Sift icing sugar and cocoa into a small bowl; gradually stir in hot butter mixture until smooth. Cover; refrigerate about 15 minutes or until frosting thickens. Beat frosting with a wooden spoon until spreadable.

We used frangelico for this recipe, but you can use any hazelnut or chocolate-flavoured liqueur you prefer.

This cake can be stored in an airtight container for up to three days. Unfrosted cake can be frozen for up to three months.

POLKA DOT
Butter Cake

PREP + COOK TIME *1 HOUR 30 MINUTES (+ REFRIGERATION & STANDING)* SERVES *14*

250g (8 ounces) unsalted butter, softened
2½ cups (550g) caster (superfine) sugar
2 teaspoons vanilla extract
6 eggs
1½ cups (225g) plain (all-purpose) flour
1½ cups (225g) self-raising flour
1 cup (250ml) milk
315g (10 ounces) white chocolate Melts
pink, yellow, blue and green food colourings

WHITE CHOCOLATE GANACHE
500g (1 pound) white eating chocolate,
   chopped coarsely
1½ cups (375ml) pouring cream

1 Preheat oven to 140°C/280°F. Grease two deep
   22cm (9-inch) round cake pans; line bases and
   sides with baking paper, extending the paper 5cm
   (2 inches) above sides.
2 Beat butter, sugar, extract, eggs, sifted flours and
   milk in a large bowl with an electric mixer on low
   speed until combined. Increase speed to medium;
   beat about 2 minutes or until mixture is smooth
   and changed to a paler colour. Spread mixture
   evenly into pans; tap gently on the bench to release
   large air bubbles.
3 Bake cakes about 1 hour. Stand in pans 5 minutes;
   turn, top-side up, onto wire racks to cool.
4 Meanwhile, make white chocolate ganache.

5 Place white chocolate Melts in a small heatproof
   bowl over a small saucepan of simmering water;
   stir until melted. Divide chocolate into four small
   bowls; tint chocolate with colourings.
6 Working with one colour at a time, spoon chocolate
   into small piping bags. Pipe small, medium and
   large discs onto a baking-paper-lined tray; tap tray
   gently on the bench to flatten rounds. Stand at
   room temperature until set.
7 Level top of cakes. Place one cake on a cake stand
   or prepared cake board (see notes); spread with
   one-third of the ganache, top with other cake.
   Spread remaining ganache all over cake. Decorate
   with chocolate discs.

WHITE CHOCOLATE GANACHE
Stir ingredients in a large heatproof bowl over a
large saucepan of simmering water until smooth.
Cover; refrigerate about 3 hours or until thick.
Beat ganache in a large bowl with electric mixer
until firm peaks form.

Use small piping bags without a tube or strong
plastic bags – snip a tiny corner from the bag for
easy piping.
Prepared cake boards are available from cake
decorating and craft stores. You will need one
30cm (12-inch) round board for this cake.
This cake can be made a day ahead; keep in the
refrigerator. Plain cakes can be frozen for up to
three months.

RASPBERRY LAYERED
Butterfly Cake
(RECIPE PAGES 308 & 309)

RASPBERRY LAYERED
Butterfly Cake

PREP + COOK TIME *2 HOURS 20 MINUTES (+ STANDING)* **SERVES** *10*

185g (6 ounces) white eating chocolate,
   chopped coarsely
90g (3 ounces) unsalted butter,
   chopped coarsely
1 cup (250ml) buttermilk
1¼ cups (275g) caster (superfine) sugar
3 eggs
1 teaspoon vanilla extract
1 cup (150g) plain (all-purpose) flour
½ cup (75g) self-raising flour
½ teaspoon bicarbonate of soda (baking soda)
125g (4 ounces) white chocolate Melts

FLUFFY MOCK CREAM FROSTING
⅓ cup (80ml) milk
⅔ cup (160ml) water
2 cups (440g) caster (superfine) sugar
2 teaspoons gelatine
⅓ cup (80ml) water, extra
500g (1 pound) unsalted butter, softened
2 teaspoons vanilla extract
¼ cup (80g) raspberry jam, warmed,
   strained, cooled
pink food colouring

1. Preheat oven to 150°C/300°F. Grease two 17cm (6¾-inch) round cake pans; line bases and sides with baking paper, extending the paper 5cm (2 inches) above sides.

2. Stir chocolate, butter and buttermilk in a medium saucepan over low heat until smooth. Transfer to a large bowl; cool 10 minutes.

3. Whisk sugar, eggs and extract into chocolate mixture. Whisk in sifted dry ingredients until mixture is smooth and glossy. Divide mixture evenly into pans.

4. Bake cakes about 1 hour. Stand in pans 5 minutes; turn, top-side up, onto wire racks to cool.

5. Make fluffy mock cream frosting. Transfer half the frosting to a medium bowl, stir in jam; tint pink with colouring.

6. Draw butterflies onto baking paper (we used one large, one medium and five small butterflies); place paper, marked-side down, onto an oven tray.

7. Place white chocolate Melts in a small heatproof bowl over a small saucepan of simmering water; stir until melted. Tint melted chocolate pink; spoon into a piping bag. Pipe chocolate around and inside butterfly shapes on tray; stand at room temperature until set.

8. Split cold cakes in half; sandwich cakes with pink frosting on a cake stand or prepared cake board (see notes). Spread cake all over with remaining plain frosting. Position butterflies on cake.

FLUFFY MOCK CREAM FROSTING

Stir milk, the water and sugar in a medium saucepan over heat, without boiling, until sugar dissolves. Sprinkle gelatine over the extra water in a cup, add to pan; stir syrup until gelatine is dissolved. Cool to room temperature. Beat butter and extract in a medium bowl with an electric mixer until as white as possible. With motor operating, gradually pour in cold syrup in thin, steady stream; beat until light and fluffy. Mixture will thicken more on standing.

Use small piping bags with or without small plain tubes, or use strong plastic bags – snip a tiny corner from the bag for easy piping.
Prepared cake boards are available from cake decorating and craft stores. You will need one 20cm (8-inch) round board for this cake.
The cake can be baked two days ahead (or baked then frozen for up to three months). Fill and decorate the cake on the day of serving.

(PHOTOGRAPH PAGES 306 & 307)

CHOCOLATE *Cake*

PREP + COOK TIME *1 HOUR 45 MINUTES (+ REFRIGERATION)* **SERVES** *10*

185g (6 ounces) dark eating (semi-sweet)
   chocolate, chopped coarsely
⅓ cup (35g) cocoa powder
1⅔ cups (410ml) boiling water
250g (8 ounces) unsalted butter, softened
2 cups (440g) firmly packed dark brown sugar
4 eggs
1 teaspoon vanilla extract
¾ cup (180g) sour cream
1 cup (150g) plain (all-purpose) flour
1 cup (150g) self-raising flour
1 teaspoon bicarbonate of soda (baking soda)

MILK CHOCOLATE GANACHE

700g (1½ pounds) milk eating chocolate,
   chopped coarsely
1⅔ cups (410ml) pouring cream

1 Preheat oven to 140°C/280°F. Grease two deep
   20cm (8-inch) round cake pans; line bases and
   sides with baking paper.
2 Stir chocolate, sifted cocoa and the water in a
   medium saucepan over low heat until smooth.
   Transfer mixture to a large bowl; cool 15 minutes.
3 Add butter, sugar, eggs, extract, sour cream and
   sifted dry ingredients to chocolate mixture; beat
   on low speed with electric mixer until combined.
   Increase speed to medium; beat about 3 minutes
   or until mixture is smooth and changed to a paler
   colour. Spread mixture evenly into pans.

4 Bake cakes about 1¼ hours. Stand in pans 5 minutes;
   turn, top-side up, onto wire racks to cool.
5 Meanwhile, make milk chocolate ganache.
6 Split cakes in half; sandwich cakes using about
   ½ cup of the ganache between each layer. Position
   cake on a cake stand or prepared cake board (see
   notes), secure with a little ganache. Spread cake all
   over with remaining ganache.

MILK CHOCOLATE GANACHE

Stir ingredients in a large heatproof bowl over a
large saucepan of simmering water until smooth.
Cover; refrigerate 3 hours or until thick. Beat
ganache in a large bowl with an electric mixer
until firm peaks form.

Prepared cake boards are available from cake
decorating and craft stores. You will need one
25cm (10-inch) round board for this cake.
The cake and ganache can be made a day ahead.
Store cake in an airtight container. Whip ganache
and assemble cake up to an hour before serving.
Plain cakes can be frozen for up to three months.

PINK VELVET
Cake

PREP + COOK TIME *1 HOUR* (+ COOLING & FREEZING) SERVES *12*

125g (4 ounces) butter, softened

1½ cups (330g) caster (superfine) sugar

1 teaspoon vanilla extract

2 eggs

1½ cups (225g) plain (all-purpose) flour

2 tablespoons cornflour (cornstarch)

2 tablespoons cocoa powder

1 cup (250ml) buttermilk

1 tablespoon rose pink food colouring

1 teaspoon white vinegar

1 teaspoon bicarbonate of soda (baking soda)

1 cup (50g) flaked coconut

MASCARPONE FROSTING

250g (8 ounces) cream cheese, softened

250g (8 ounces) mascarpone cheese

1 cup (160g) icing (confectioners') sugar

1 teaspoon vanilla extract

1¼ cups (310ml) thickened (heavy) cream
(see notes)

1 Preheat oven to 180°C/350°F. Grease two deep 22cm (9-inch) round cake pans; line bases and sides with baking paper.

2 Beat butter, sugar, extract and eggs in a small bowl with an electric mixer until light and fluffy. Transfer mixture to a large bowl; stir in sifted flours and cocoa, and combined buttermilk and food colouring, in two batches.

3 Combine vinegar and soda in a cup; allow to fizz, then fold into cake mixture. Divide mixture into pans.

4 Bake cakes about 25 minutes. Stand in pans 10 minutes; turn, top-side up, onto a wire rack to cool. Enclose cakes in plastic wrap; freeze 40 minutes.

5 Meanwhile, make mascarpone frosting.

6 Split cold cakes in half. Place one layer on a serving plate, cut-side up; spread with ⅔ cup frosting. Repeat layering, finishing with remaining frosting spread over top and side of cake; press coconut onto side of cake.

MASCARPONE FROSTING

Beat cream cheese, mascarpone, icing sugar and extract in a small bowl with an electric mixer until smooth. Beat in cream.

You can use just one 300ml carton of cream for this recipe.

Plain cake can be frozen for up to three months.

Cake can be filled and decorated up to eight hours before serving; keep in the fridge.

MIXED BERRY
and Ricotta Tart

PREP + COOK TIME *1 HOUR 30 MINUTES (+ REFRIGERATION)* **SERVES** *10*

1⅓ cups (200g) plain (all-purpose) flour
185g (6 ounces) cold butter, chopped coarsely
¼ cup (60ml) iced water, approximately
500g (1 pound) soft ricotta cheese
⅓ cup (80ml) pouring cream
⅓ cup (75g) caster (superfine) sugar
3 eggs
1 tablespoon finely grated lemon rind
200g (6½ ounces) strawberries, halved
125g (4 ounces) blueberries
125g (4 ounces) raspberries
1 teaspoon icing (confectioners') sugar

1 Sift flour into a large bowl; rub in butter until crumbly. Mix in enough of the water to make ingredients just come together. Knead dough lightly on a floured surface until smooth. Flatten pastry slightly, wrap in plastic wrap; refrigerate 30 minutes.

2 Grease a 22cm (9-inch) round loose-based fluted flan pan. Roll out pastry on a floured surface or between sheets of baking paper until large enough to line pan. Ease pastry into pan; press over base and side, trim excess pastry. Prick base all over with a fork; refrigerate 30 minutes.

3 Preheat oven to 200°C/400°F.

4 Place pan on an oven tray, line pastry with baking paper; fill with dried beans or rice. Bake 15 minutes. Remove paper and beans; bake a further 10 minutes or until browned lightly and crisp. Cool.

5 Reduce oven to 180°C/350°F.

6 Meanwhile, beat ricotta, cream, caster sugar, eggs and rind in a small bowl with an electric mixer until smooth. Pour mixture into tart shell.

7 Bake tart about 35 minutes or until filling is just set. Refrigerate until cold.

8 Just before serving, top tart with berries; dust with sifted icing sugar.

You can also make the pastry using a food processor. Process flour and butter until crumbly; with motor operating, add the water and process until ingredients just come together. You can also use ready-made shortcrust pastry.
This tart is best made on the day of serving.

CHOCOLATE
Chiffon Cake

PREP + COOK TIME *1 HOUR 30 MINUTES* **SERVES** *16*

½ cup (50g) cocoa powder
¾ cup (180ml) boiling water
2 cups (300g) self-raising flour
1½ cups (330g) caster (superfine) sugar
7 eggs, separated
½ cup (125ml) vegetable oil
1 teaspoon vanilla extract

WALNUT PRALINE
1 cup (220g) caster (superfine) sugar
½ cup (50g) walnuts
60g (2 ounces) dark eating (semi-sweet)
   chocolate, chopped coarsely

BRANDIED BUTTERCREAM
190g (6 ounces) butter, softened
3 cups (480g) icing (confectioners') sugar
¼ cup (25g) cocoa powder
¼ cup (60ml) brandy

1 Preheat oven to 180°C/350°F. Grease a deep 22cm (9-inch) round cake pan; line base and side with baking paper.
2 Blend cocoa with the water in a small bowl; cool. Sift flour and sugar into a large bowl; add cocoa mixture, egg yolks, oil and extract. Beat with an electric mixer until smooth and mixture is changed to a paler colour.
3 Beat egg whites in a large bowl with an electric mixer until soft peaks form; fold into cocoa mixture, in four batches. Pour mixture into pan.
4 Bake cake about 1 hour. Stand in pan 5 minutes; turn, top-side up, onto a wire rack to cool.
5 Make walnut praline, then brandied buttercream.
6 Split cold cake into three layers; join layers with some of the buttercream. Spread top and sides of cake evenly with remaining buttercream. Decorate with walnut praline. Serve immediately.

WALNUT PRALINE
Place sugar in a heavy-based frying pan; cook over heat, without stirring, until sugar is melted and golden brown. Add nuts; pour onto a greased oven tray. Cool. Blend or process praline with chocolate until finely chopped.

BRANDIED BUTTERCREAM
Beat butter in a small bowl with an electric mixer until as white as possible; beat in sifted icing sugar and cocoa, then brandy.

To decorate the side of the cake with praline (as pictured), spread just the side of the filled cake with buttercream. Hold the top and the bottom of the cake in your hands and roll the cake – like a wheel – in the praline. Place the cake on a serving plate, then spread the top with remaining buttercream. This cake is best made on the day of serving.

BANANA CARAMEL
Layer Cake

(RECIPE PAGE 320)

BANANA CARAMEL
Layer Cake

PREP + COOK TIME *1 HOUR 10 MINUTES* SERVES *8*

185g (6 ounces) butter, softened
1¼ cup (175g) caster (superfine) sugar
3 eggs
2¼ cups (335g) self-raising flour
½ teaspoon bicarbonate of soda (baking soda)
1¼ cups mashed banana
⅓ cup (80ml) milk
¾ cup (180ml) thickened (heavy) cream
395g (12½ ounces) canned caramel top 'n' fill
1 large banana (230g), sliced thinly
1 tablespoon icing (confectioners') sugar

1 Preheat oven to 180°C/350°F. Grease a 24cm (9½-inch) bundt pan or 24cm (9½-inch) patterned silicone pan well with butter.
2 Beat butter and caster sugar in a small bowl with an electric mixer until light and fluffy. Beat in eggs, one at a time. Transfer mixture to a large bowl; stir in sifted dry ingredients, mashed banana and milk. Spread mixture into pan.
3 Bake cake about 40 minutes. Stand in pan 5 minutes; turn onto a wire rack to cool.
4 Beat cream in a small bowl with an electric mixer until firm peaks form.
5 Split cake into three layers. Spread bottom layer of cake with half the caramel; top with half the banana slices, then half the cream. Repeat next layer using remaining caramel, banana slices and cream. Replace top of cake. Dust with sifted icing sugar. Serve immediately.

You need two large overripe bananas (460g) for the amount of mashed banana used in this recipe. Plain cake can be frozen for up to three months.

(PHOTOGRAPH PAGE 319)

MINI FRUIT MINCE
Cakes

PREP + COOK TIME *40 MINUTES (+ COOLING)* MAKES *40*

1⅓ cups (200g) self-raising flour
⅓ cup (75g) firmly packed light brown sugar
1½ cups (440g) fruit mince
½ cup (125ml) olive oil
⅓ cup (80ml) milk
1 egg
250g (8 ounces) white ready-made icing
¼ cup (40g) pure icing (confectioners') sugar
cachous

1 Preheat oven to 200°C/400°F. Line 40 holes of four 12-hole (1-tablespoon/20ml) mini muffin pans with paper cases.
2 Sift flour and brown sugar into a large bowl.
3 Whisk fruit mince, oil, milk and egg in a medium bowl until combined; stir into flour mixture until barely combined. Drop level tablespoons of mixture into paper cases.
4 Bake cakes about 15 minutes. Cool in pans.
5 Knead icing on a surface dusted with sifted icing sugar until smooth. Roll out icing until 3mm (⅛ inch) thick; cut out stars (see notes). Brush a tiny amount of water onto the backs of stars; position on cakes. Press cachous into centres of stars before icing dries.

We used 1.5cm (¾-inch), 2.5cm (1-inch) and 3cm (1¼-inch) star-shaped cutters.
Using store-bought fruit mince means these cakes are quick and simple to make – perfect for when last-minute guests pop in over the festive season. These cakes will keep in an airtight container at room temperature for up to a week. Plain cakes can be frozen for up to three months.

MINI FRUIT MINCE
Cakes

BUTTERY LIGHT FRUIT CAKE
with Almond Crumble

PREP + COOK TIME *2 HOURS 15 MINUTES (+ STANDING & COOLING)* SERVES *12*

1 cup (160g) sultanas
½ cup (85g) coarsely chopped raisins
½ cup (125g) coarsely chopped glacé peaches
½ cup (125g) coarsely chopped glacé apricots
¼ cup (60g) coarsely chopped glacé orange rind
¼ cup (50g) coarsely chopped red glacé cherries
½ cup (125ml) orange-flavoured liqueur
185g (6 ounces) butter, softened
1 cup (220g) caster (superfine) sugar
2 teaspoons vanilla extract
2 eggs
⅓ cup (80g) sour cream
¾ cup (90g) ground almonds
¾ cup (110g) plain (all-purpose) flour
⅓ cup (50g) self-raising flour

ALMOND CRUMBLE
½ cup (75g) plain (all-purpose) flour
60g (2 ounces) butter
2 tablespoons firmly packed light brown sugar
90g (3 ounces) marzipan or almond paste
½ cup (40g) natural sliced almonds

1   Combine fruit and liqueur in a large bowl. Cover; stand about 1 hour or until most of the liquid is absorbed. Stir well.
2   Make almond crumble.
3   Preheat oven to 150°C/300°F. Grease a deep 14cm x 23cm (5½-inch x 9¼-inch) loaf pan; line base and sides with two thicknesses of baking paper, extending the paper 5cm (2 inches) above sides.
4   Beat butter, sugar and extract in a small bowl with an electric mixer until combined. Beat in eggs, one at a time; beat in sour cream. Stir butter mixture into fruit mixture, then stir in ground almonds and sifted flours. Spoon mixture into pan; smooth surface. Sprinkle with almond crumble.
5   Bake cake about 1¾ hours. Cover with foil; cool cake in pan.

ALMOND CRUMBLE
Place flour in a medium bowl; rub in butter until crumbly. Stir in sugar, crumbled marzipan and nuts.

Use Cointreau, Grand Marnier or curaçao for a citrus-flavoured liqueur.
This cake will keep in an airtight container at room temperature for up to four weeks. It can be frozen for up to three months.

DELUXE CHOCOLATE
Cupcake Tower

PREP + COOK TIME 1 HOUR 40 MINUTES PER BATCH (+ COOLING) MAKES 120

MOCHA MUD CAKES

500g (1 pound) butter, chopped coarsely

280g (9 ounces) dark eating (semi-sweet)
    chocolate, chopped coarsely

4 cups (880g) caster (superfine) sugar

2 cups (500ml) water

⅔ cup (160ml) coffee liqueur

2 tablespoons instant coffee granules

3 cups (450g) plain (all-purpose) flour

½ cup (75g) self-raising flour

½ cup (50g) cocoa powder

4 eggs

CHOCOLATE GANACHE

2⅓ cups (580ml) thickened (heavy) cream

750g (1½ pounds) milk eating chocolate,
    chopped coarsely

DECORATIONS

200g (6½ ounces) white eating chocolate

½ cup (115g) finely chopped glacé ginger

¼ cup (25g) roasted coffee beans

1 Preheat oven to 170°C/340°F. Line two 12-hole (⅓-cup/80ml) muffin pans with paper cases.

2 For the mocha mud cakes, stir butter, chocolate, sugar, the water, liqueur and coffee in a large saucepan over low heat until smooth. Transfer mixture to a large bowl; cool 15 minutes.

3 Whisk sifted flours and cocoa into chocolate mixture, then whisk in eggs.

4 Pour ¼ cup of mixture into each paper case. Bake cakes about 40 minutes. Stand cakes in pans 5 minutes; turn, top-side up, onto wire racks to cool.

5 Repeat step 4 with remaining mixture before starting on the next batch.

6 Make chocolate ganache.

7 Spread cold cakes with ganache. Run a vegetable peeler down the side of white chocolate block to make chocolate curls. Decorate cakes with curls, ginger and coffee beans. Arrange cakes in tiers on a cake stand.

CHOCOLATE GANACHE

Bring cream to the boil in a small saucepan; remove from heat. When bubbles subside, pour over chocolate in a medium heatproof bowl; stir until smooth. Cover; refrigerate 30 minutes or until ganache is spreadable.

You need to buy triple the quantity of the ingredients for the mocha mud cake recipe. You will need to make three separate batches – do not double or triple this recipe. It's important to measure the cake mixture carefully so the cakes are all the same depth. The mixture will be fine standing at room temperature while you bake the cakes in batches. Each batch will make 40 cakes. You need 120 standard muffin paper cases. Plain cakes can be frozen for up to three months. Assemble the tower up to four hours before serving.

ORANGE MARMALADE
and Cranberry Cake

PREP + COOK TIME *2 HOURS 30 MINUTES (+ STANDING & COOLING)* **SERVES** *12*

1 cup (130g) dried cranberries
1 cup (250ml) orange-flavoured liqueur
1 large orange (300g)
1 cup (250ml) water
1½ cups (330g) caster (superfine) sugar
185g (6 ounces) butter, softened
3 eggs
1 cup (120g) ground almonds
1 cup (150g) plain (all-purpose) flour
½ cup (75g) self-raising flour

CRANBERRY GLAZE
3 cups (480g) pure icing (confectioners') sugar
¼ cup (60ml) cranberry juice, approximately

1 Combine cranberries and liqueur in a small bowl; cover, stand overnight.

2 Meanwhile, cut unpeeled orange into eight wedges; slice wedges thinly crossways. Place fruit and seeds (if any) in a small bowl, add the water; cover, stand overnight.

3 Transfer orange mixture to a medium saucepan; bring to the boil. Reduce heat; simmer, covered, stirring occasionally, about 40 minutes or until rind is tender. Add sugar to pan; stir over high heat, without boiling, until sugar dissolves. Bring to the boil; boil, uncovered, stirring occasionally, about 20 minutes or until marmalade jells when tested. Strain marmalade through sieve into a small heatproof bowl; reserve marmalade and rind mixtures separately. Cool.

4 Preheat oven to 150°C/300°F. Grease a 20cm (8-inch) baba or fluted ring pan well; sprinkle with flour, shake out excess.

5 Beat butter and marmalade in a small bowl with an electric mixer until combined. Beat in eggs, one at a time. (Mixture may separate at this stage but will come together later.) Transfer mixture to a large bowl; stir in ground almonds, sifted flours, cranberry mixture and rind mixture. Spread mixture into pan.

6 Bake cake about 1¼ hours. Stand in pan 5 minutes; turn onto a wire rack to cool.

7 Meanwhile, make cranberry glaze.

8 Drizzle cold cake with glaze.

CRANBERRY GLAZE

Sift icing sugar into a medium bowl; stir in enough juice to make a stiff paste. Stir mixture over a medium saucepan of simmering water until glaze is spreadable.

Use Cointreau, Grand Marnier or curaçao for a citrus-flavoured liqueur.
The iced cake will keep in an airtight container at room temperature for up to one week. Uniced cake can be frozen for up to three months.

JAM SHORTBREAD
Snowflakes

PREP + COOK TIME *1 HOUR 30 MINUTES* *(+ REFRIGERATION & STANDING)* MAKES *20*

250g (8 ounces) butter, softened
1 teaspoon vanilla extract
1¼ cups (200g) icing (confectioners') sugar
2⅓ cups (350g) plain (all-purpose) flour
½ cup (75g) wheaten cornflour (cornstarch)
2 tablespoons milk
½ cup (160g) jam
2 tablespoons icing (confectioners') sugar, extra

1 Beat butter, extract and sifted icing sugar in a small bowl with an electric mixer until light and fluffy. Transfer mixture to a large bowl; stir in sifted flour and cornflour, and milk, in two batches. Divide dough in half, enclose in plastic wrap; refrigerate 30 minutes.

2 Preheat oven to 160°C/325°F. Line oven trays with baking paper.

3 Roll one half of the dough between sheets of baking paper until 3mm (⅛ inch) thick. Cut out snowflakes using a 9.5cm (4-inch) snowflake cutter, re-rolling scraps. Place shortbread, about 2.5cm (1 inch) apart, on trays. Repeat with remaining dough. Cut out the centre of half the snowflakes using a 6cm (2½-inch) snowflake cutter. Refrigerate 15 minutes.

4 Bake shortbread 10 minutes. Stand 10 minutes; spread large shortbreads with 1 teaspoon jam. Top with snowflake cut outs. Bake a further 5 minutes.

5 Dust shortbread with sifted extra icing sugar before serving (see notes).

To make a neat job of dusting the icing sugar on the snowflakes, position the smaller cutter in the centre of each snowflake, cover the top of the cutter with a piece of foil to protect the jam. Dust the snowflake with the extra sifted icing sugar.

If you don't have a set of snowflake cutters, you could use star cutters instead.

We used an assortment of jams – black cherry, raspberry and apricot. You can use any flavoured jam you like.

Shortbread will keep in an airtight container at room temperature for up to four days.

KOUGLOF

PREP + COOK TIME *1 HOUR 15 MINUTES (+ STANDING)* **SERVES** *20*

½ cup (75g) raisins
¼ cup (60ml) kirsch
2 teaspoons finely grated orange rind
16 almond kernels
3⅓ cups (500g) plain (all-purpose) flour
1 teaspoon coarse cooking salt (kosher salt)
½ cup (110g) caster (superfine) sugar
4 teaspoons (14g) dried yeast
¾ cup (180ml) warm milk
4 eggs
200g (6½ ounces) unsalted butter,
   chopped finely, softened
½ cup (70g) slivered almonds
2 teaspoons icing (confectioners') sugar

1. Combine raisins, kirsch and rind in a small bowl.
2. Grease a 24cm (9½-inch) (top measurement) kouglof pan well. Place almond kernels in the grooves of the pan; refrigerate pan.
3. Sift flour and salt into a large bowl of an electric mixer with a dough hook attached; add caster sugar, yeast, milk and eggs. Knead on a low speed about 1 minute or until mixture forms a soft dough. Add butter. Increase speed to medium; knead about 10 minutes or until dough is smooth and elastic. Add raisin mixture and slivered almonds; knead until combined. Cover bowl; stand in a warm place about 1 hour or until dough has doubled in size.
4. Punch down dough; knead with electric mixer 1 minute. Gently push dough into pan, to avoid disturbing the nuts. Cover; stand in a warm place about 1 hour or until dough has doubled in size.
5. Meanwhile, preheat oven to 180°C/350°F.
6. Bake kouglof about 40 minutes. Stand in pan 5 minutes, before turning onto a wire rack to cool. Serve dusted with sifted icing sugar.

You will need an electric mixer fitted with a dough hook for this recipe as the dough is too soft to knead by hand.

This is a traditional cake from north-eastern France; you find similar cakes in Germany, Austria and eastern Europe (the names vary slightly: Kugelhopf, Gugelhupf). It is traditionally baked in a circular pan with a central tube made of enamelled pottery but you can easily find metal pans in cooking stores. This cake will keep in an airtight container at room temperature for about a week.

SERVING SUGGESTION

Serve warm with whipped cream. It keeps well and is delicious the following day thickly sliced, toasted and spread with butter and jam.

PFEFFERNÜSSEN

PREP + COOK TIME *35 MINUTES (+ COOLING)* **MAKES** *30*

125g (4 ounces) butter, chopped coarsely
¾ cup (165g) firmly packed light brown sugar
⅓ cup (125g) molasses
1 egg
2⅓ cups (350g) plain (all-purpose) flour
1 teaspoon ground cinnamon
½ teaspoon ground allspice
½ teaspoon finely grated nutmeg
¼ teaspoon ground cloves
¼ teaspoon finely ground black pepper
¼ teaspoon bicarbonate of soda (baking soda)
⅓ cup (55g) icing (confectioners') sugar

1 Preheat oven to 160°C/325°F. Line two oven trays with baking paper.
2 Melt butter in a small saucepan; stir in brown sugar and molasses until combined. Transfer to a large bowl; cool 10 minutes. Stir in egg, then sifted flour, spices, pepper and soda.
3 Roll level tablespoons of mixture into balls. Place balls, about 3cm (1¼ inches) apart, on trays.
4 Bake biscuits about 15 minutes or until firm to touch. Stand on trays 10 minutes.
5 Sift icing sugar into a small bowl; toss warm biscuits in sugar until well coated. Place biscuits on a wire rack to cool.

Pfeffernüssen translates from German as "pepper nut" biscuits, they are a variation on a type of German gingerbread known as "lebkuchen". Pfeffernüssen are extremely hard when they are first baked and benefit from being dunked into liquid before eating, however, they do start to soften after a day or two.
These biscuits will keep in an airtight container at room temperature for up to three weeks.

CHRISTMAS PUDDING
Cookies

PREP + COOK TIME *40 MINUTES (+ REFRIGERATION & STANDING)* MAKES *24*

60g (2 ounces) butter, softened
¼ cup (55g) caster (superfine) sugar
½ teaspoon vanilla extract
1 egg
1 cup (150g) plain (all-purpose) flour
2 tablespoons cocoa powder
24 large white and pink marshmallows (150g)
300g (9½ ounces) dark eating (semi-sweet)
   chocolate
150g (4½ ounces) white chocolate Melts
12 red glacé cherries
6 green glacé cherries

1 Beat butter, sugar, extract and egg in a small bowl with an electric mixer until combined. Stir in sifted flour and cocoa. Enclose dough in plastic wrap; refrigerate 30 minutes.
2 Preheat oven to 180°C/350°F. Grease two oven trays; line with baking paper.
3 Roll dough between sheets of baking paper until 5mm (¼ inch) thick. Using a 4.5cm (1¾-inch) round cutter, cut 24 rounds from dough, re-rolling scraps as necessary. Place rounds about 2.5cm (1 inch) apart on trays.
4 Bake cookies 10 minutes. Remove from oven, immediately press one marshmallow on top of each hot cookie. Return to oven for 1 minute. Cool on trays.

5 Melt dark chocolate in a small heatproof bowl over a small saucepan of simmering water (don't let water touch base of bowl).
6 Place cookies on a wire rack over a baking-paper-lined tray. Spoon chocolate over biscuits to completely cover marshmallows. Stand at room temperature until chocolate sets.
7 Melt white chocolate Melts in a small heatproof bowl over a small saucepan of simmering water.
8 Cut red cherries in half. Cut each green cherry into eight wedges. Working with one cookie at a time, spoon a small amount of white chocolate on top; position one red cherry half and two green cherry wedges on top. Stand at room temperature until set.

These cookies will keep, in a single layer, in an airtight container, at a cool room temperature, for up to a week.
These homemade treats make charming Christmas gifts. Arrange them in a pretty box, and tie it with a red ribbon.

GLUTEN- AND DAIRY-FREE
Spicy Fruit Cakes

PREP + COOK TIME *35 MINUTES* MAKES *12*

⅓ cup (45g) slivered almonds
½ cup (105g) finely chopped mixed
   glacé cherries
2 tablespoons finely chopped glacé ginger
¼ cup (75g) finely chopped glacé pear
100g (3 ounces) dairy-free spread
1 cup (135g) gluten-free self-raising flour
1 teaspoon ground ginger
½ teaspoon ground cloves
½ cup (110g) firmly packed light brown sugar
¼ cup (60ml) rice milk
1 egg
1 egg white

1 Preheat oven to 180°C/350°F. Grease a 12-hole (⅓-cup/80ml) standard muffin pan; line base of pan holes with rounds of baking paper (see notes).

2 Combine nuts and glacé fruit in a small bowl; sprinkle mixture evenly into pan holes.

3 Beat spread in a small bowl with an electric mixer for 1 second, just to soften slightly (see notes). Sift flour, spices and 2 tablespoons of the sugar together. Beat flour mixture and milk into spread only until combined.

4 Beat egg and egg white in a small bowl with an electric mixer about 5 minutes or until thick and creamy. Add remaining sugar, beat until dissolved. Gradually beat egg mixture into flour mixture. Spoon mixture into pan holes.

5 Bake cakes about 15 minutes. Stand in pan 5 minutes; turn, bottom-side up, onto a wire rack to cool. Remove lining papers.

The easiest way to line the base of a pan hole is to cut the bottom out of cupcake paper cases; use the correct sized case for the muffin pan. Don't overbeat the dairy-free spread or it will break down; you just need to break it up before adding the flour mixture.
These cakes will keep in an airtight container at room temperature for up to three days.
Filled with fruits, nuts and spices these fruit cakes contain all the best things about Christmas – without gluten or dairy. They are so delicious and delightfully rich that you won't feel like you're missing out on anything.

NUTTY CHOC-CHIP
Boiled Fruit Cakes

PREP + COOK TIME *2 HOURS (+ COOLING & STANDING)* MAKES *6*

185g (6 ounces) butter, chopped coarsely

2¼ cups (375g) sultanas

1½ cups (250g) coarsely chopped raisins

½ cup (140g) peanut butter

1 cup (220g) firmly packed dark brown sugar

1 cup (250ml) hazelnut- or chocolate-flavoured liqueur

180g (5½ ounces) dark eating (semi-sweet) chocolate, chopped coarsely

½ cup (70g) roasted unsalted peanuts, chopped coarsely

¾ cup (120g) almond kernels, chopped coarsely

½ cup (50g) roasted walnuts, chopped coarsely

¾ cup (110g) roasted unsalted macadamias, chopped coarsely

4 eggs, beaten lightly

1¾ cups (360g) plain (all-purpose) flour

¼ cup (35g) self-raising flour

½ cup (70g) roasted unsalted peanuts, extra

½ cup (80g) almond kernels, extra

½ cup (50g) roasted walnuts, extra

½ cup (70g) roasted unsalted macadamias, extra

TOFFEE

1½ cups (330g) caster (superfine) sugar

½ cup (125ml) water

1 Place butter in a large saucepan with fruit, peanut butter, sugar and liqueur; stir over heat, without boiling, until sugar dissolves. Bring to the boil. Reduce heat; simmer, covered, 10 minutes. Transfer mixture to a large bowl. Cool.

2 Preheat oven to 130°C/260°F. Grease six deep 10cm (4-inch) square cake pans; line base and sides with two thicknesses of baking paper, extending the paper 5cm (2 inches) above sides.

3 Stir chocolate and chopped nuts into fruit mixture with eggs and sifted flours. Spread mixture into pans.

4 Bake cakes about 1 hour. Cover hot cakes with foil; turn cakes upside-down. Cool in pans overnight.

5 Make toffee.

6 Coarsely chop extra nuts. Drizzle one of the cakes with a little toffee; press some of the nuts on top. Drizzle with a little more toffee to glaze. Repeat with remaining cakes, toffee and nuts. Stand until set.

TOFFEE

Stir sugar and the water in small saucepan over high heat, without boiling, until sugar dissolves. Bring to the boil; boil, uncovered, without stirring, about 10 minutes or until caramel in colour.

Use frangelico (hazelnut-flavoured liqueur) or crème de cacao (chocolate-flavoured liqueur). Use a serrated knife to cut the cakes. These cakes will keep in an airtight container at room temperature for four weeks; the toffee will soften after a few days, depending on the weather.

GLOSSARY

ALLSPICE also known as pimento or jamaican pepper; so-named because it tastes like a combination of nutmeg, cumin, clove and cinnamon. Available whole (a dark-brown berry the size of a pea) or ground, and used in both sweet and savoury dishes.

ALMONDS flat, pointy-tipped nuts having a pitted brown shell enclosing a creamy white kernel which is covered by a brown skin.
blanched brown skins removed.
essence made with almond oil and alcohol or another agent.
flaked paper-thin slices.
ground also known as almond meal.
slivered small pieces cut lengthways
vienna toffee-coated almonds.

BAKE BLIND a cooking term to describe baking a pie shell or pastry case before filling is added. If a filling does not need to be baked or is very wet, you may need to "blind-bake" the unfilled shell. To bake blind, ease the pastry into a pan or dish, place on an oven tray; line the pastry with baking paper then fill with dried beans, uncooked rice or "baking beans" (also called pie weights). Bake according to the recipe's directions then cool before adding the suggested filling.

BAKING PAPER also called parchment paper or baking parchment – is a silicone-coated paper that is primarily used for lining baking pans and oven trays so cakes and biscuits won't stick, making removal easy.

BAKING POWDER a raising agent consisting mainly of two parts cream of tartar to one part bicarbonate of soda (baking soda).

BAY LEAVES aromatic leaves from the bay tree available fresh or dried; adds a strong, slightly peppery flavour.

BICARBONATE OF SODA (BAKING SODA) a raising agent.

BISCUITS also called cookies; almost always an "eat-in-your-hand"-sized soft or crisp sweet cake.
butternut snap crunchy biscuit made from rolled oats, coconut and golden syrup.
plain sweet crisp, sweet and vanilla flavoured.

BRANDY short for brandywine, the translation of the Dutch "brandwijn", burnt wine. A general term for a liqueur distilled from wine grapes (usually white), it is used as the basis for many sweet-to-dry spirits made with fruits. Cognac and Armagnac are two of the finest aged brandies available.

BREAD
brioche French in origin; a rich, yeast-leavened, cake-like bread made with butter and eggs. Available from cake or specialty bread shops.
ciabatta in Italian, the word means slipper, the traditional shape of this popular crisp-crusted, open-textured white sourdough bread. A good bread to use for bruschetta.

BRUISE a cooking term to describe the slight crushing given to aromatic ingredients, such as lemon grass and cardamom pods, with the flat side of a heavy knife to release flavour and aroma.

BURGHUL also called bulgar wheat; hulled steamed wheat kernels that, once dried, are crushed into various sized grains. Used in Middle Eastern dishes such as felafel, kibbeh and tabbouleh. Is not the same as cracked wheat.

BUTTER we use salted butter unless stated otherwise; 125g is equal to 1 stick (4 ounces). Unsalted or "sweet" butter has no salt added and is perhaps the most popular butter among pastry-chefs.

BUTTERMILK originally the term given to the slightly sour liquid left after butter was churned from cream, today it is made from no-fat or low-fat milk to which specific bacterial cultures have neen added. Despite its name, it is actually low in fat.

CACHOUS also called dragées in some countries; minuscule (3mm to 5mm) metallic-looking-but-edible confectionery balls used in cake decorating; available in silver, gold or various colours.

CARDAMOM a spice native to India and used extensively in its cuisine; can be purchased in pod, seed or ground form. Has a distinctive aromatic, sweetly rich flavour.

CHEESE
cheddar the most common cow-milk tasty cheese; should be aged, hard and have a pronounced bite.
cream commonly called philadelphia or philly; a soft cow-milk cheese, its fat content ranges from 14% to 33%.
fetta Greek in origin; a crumbly textured goat- or sheep-milk cheese having a sharp, salty taste. Ripened and stored in salted whey; particularly good cubed and tossed into salads.
gruyère a hard-rind Swiss cheese with small holes and a nutty, slightly salty flavour. A popular cheese for soufflés.
mascarpone an Italian fresh cultured-cream product made in much the same way as yogurt. Whiteish to creamy yellow in colour, with a buttery-rich, luscious texture. Soft, creamy and spreadable, it is used in Italian desserts and as an accompaniment to fresh fruit.
parmesan also called parmigiano; is a hard, grainy cow-milk cheese originating in Italy. Reggiano is the best variety.
ricotta a soft, sweet, moist, white cow-milk cheese with a low fat content and a slightly grainy texture. The name roughly translates as "cooked again" and refers to ricotta's manufacture from a whey that is itself a by-product of other cheese making.

CHERRIES
glacé also called candied cherries; boiled in heavy sugar syrup and then dried.
morello sour cherries available bottled in syurp. Used in baking and savoury dishes and are a good match for game.

CHOCOLATE

choc bits also known as chocolate chips or chocolate morsels; available in milk, white and dark chocolate. Made of cocoa liquor, cocoa butter, sugar and an emulsifier, these hold their shape in baking and are ideal for decorating.

couverture a term used to describe a fine quality, very rich chocolate high in both cocoa butter and cocoa liquor. Requires tempering when used to coat but not if used in baking, mousses or fillings.

dark cooking also called compounded chocolate; good for cooking as it doesn't require tempering and sets at room temperature. Made with vegetable fat instead of cocoa butter so it lacks the rich, buttery flavour of eating chocolate. Cocoa butter is the most expensive component in chocolate, so the substitution of a vegetable fat means that compounded chocolate is much cheaper to produce.

dark eating (semi-sweet) also called luxury chocolate; made of a high percentage of cocoa liquor and cocoa butter, and little added sugar. Unless stated otherwise, we use dark eating chocolate in this book as it's ideal for use in desserts and cakes.

melts small discs of compounded milk, white or dark chocolate ideal for melting and moulding.

milk most popular eating chocolate, mild and very sweet; similar in make-up to dark with the difference being the addition of milk solids.

white contains no cocoa solids but derives its sweet flavour from cocoa butter. Very sensitive to heat.

CHOCOLATE HAZELNUT SPREAD also known as Nutella; made of cocoa powder, hazelnuts, sugar and milk.

CINNAMON available in pieces (called sticks or quills) and ground into powder; one of the world's most common spices, used as a sweet, fragrant flavouring for both sweet and savoury foods.

CLOVES dried flower buds of a tropical tree; can be used whole or in ground form. They have a strong scent and taste so should be used sparingly.

COCOA POWDER also known as unsweetened cocoa; cocoa beans (cacao seeds) that have been fermented, roasted, shelled, ground into powder then cleared of most of the fat content. Unsweetened cocoa is used in hot chocolate drink mixtures; milk powder and sugar are added to the ground product.

COCONUT

desiccated concentrated, dried, unsweetened and finely shredded coconut flesh.

essence synthetically produced from flavouring, oil and alcohol.

flaked dried flaked coconut flesh.

shredded unsweetened thin strips of dried coconut flesh.

CONFECTIONERS' RICE PAPER resembling a grainy sheet of paper, this rice paper is translucent, glossy and edible. It is imported from Holland and used in confectionery making and baking. It can be bought from specialty food stores. Don't confuse this rice paper with the one used in recipes such as fresh rice paper rolls, which needs to be soaked to soften.

CORIANDER (CILANTRO) also called pak chee or chinese parsley; bright-green-leafed herb with both pungent aroma and taste. Used as an ingredient in a wide variety of cuisines. Often stirred into or sprinkled over a dish just before serving for maximum impact as, like other leafy herbs, its characteristics diminish with cooking. Both the stems and roots of coriander are used in Thai cooking: wash well before chopping. Coriander seeds are dried and sold either whole or ground, and neither form tastes remotely like the fresh leaf.

CORN FLAKES commercially manufactured cereal made of dehydrated then baked crisp flakes of corn.

CORNFLOUR (CORNSTARCH) available made from corn or wheat (wheaten cornflour, gluten-free, gives a lighter texture in cakes); used as a thickening agent in cooking.

CRANBERRIES available dried and frozen; have a rich, astringent flavour and can be used in cooking sweet and savoury dishes. The dried version can usually be substituted for or with other dried fruit.

CREAM

pouring also known as pure or fresh cream. It has no additives and contains a minimum fat content of 35%.

sour a thick, commercially-cultured sour cream with a minimum fat content of 35%.

thick (double) a dolloping cream with a minimum fat content of 45%.

thickened (heavy) a whipping cream that contains a thickener. It has a minimum fat content of 35%.

CREAM OF TARTAR the acid ingredient in baking powder; added to confectionery mixtures to help prevent sugar from crystallising. Keeps frostings creamy and improves volume when beating egg whites.

CRÈME FRAÎCHE a mature, naturally fermented cream (minimum fat content 35%) having a velvety texture and slightly tangy, nutty flavour. Crème fraîche, a French variation of sour cream, can boil without curdling and be used in sweet and savoury dishes.

CUMIN also known as zeera or comino; resembling caraway in size, cumin is the dried seed of a plant related to the parsley family. Its spicy, almost curry-like flavour is essential to the traditional foods of Mexico, India, North Africa and the Middle East. Available dried as seeds or ground.

CUSTARD POWDER instant mixture used to make pouring custard; similar to North American instant pudding mixes.

DATES fruit of the date palm tree, eaten fresh or dried, on their own or in prepared dishes. About 4cm to 6cm in length, oval and plump, thin-kinned, with a honey-sweet flavour and sticky texture. Best known, perhaps, for their inclusion in sticky toffee pudding: also found in muesli; muffins, scones and cakes; compotes and stewed fruit desserts.

DRIED CURRANTS dried tiny, almost black raisins so named from the grape type native to Corinth, Greece; most often used in jams, jellies and sauces (the best-known of which is the English cumberland sauce). These are not the same as fresh currants, which are the fruit of a plant in the gooseberry family.

EGGS we use large chicken eggs weighing an average of 60g (2 ounces). If a recipe calls for raw or barely cooked eggs, exercise caution if there is a salmonella problem in your area, particularly in food eaten by children and pregnant women.

EGGWASH beaten egg (white, yolk or both) and milk or water; often brushed over pastry or bread to impart colour or gloss.

ESSENCE/EXTRACT an essence is either a distilled concentration of a food quality or an artificial creation of it. Coconut and almond essences are synthetically produced substances used in small amounts to impart their respective flavours to foods. An extract is made by actually extracting the flavour from a food product. In the case of vanilla, pods are soaked, usually in alcohol, to capture the authentic flavour. Essences and extracts keep indefinitely if stored in a cool dark place.

FIGS are best eaten in peak season, at the height of summer. They vary in skin and flesh colour according to type not ripeness. When ripe, figs should be unblemished and bursting with flesh; nectar beads at the base indicate when a fig is at its best. Figs are also glacéd, dried or canned in sugar syrup; these are usually sold at health-food stores, Middle Eastern food shops or specialty cheese counters.

FLOUR
baker's also known as gluten-enriched, strong or bread-mix flour. Produced from a variety of what has a high gluten (protein) content and is best suited for pizza and bread making: the expansion caused by the yeast and the stretchiness imposed by kneading require a flour that is "strong" enough to handle these stresses. Since domestic breadmakers entered the marketplace, it has become easier to find strong flour; look for it at your supermarket or health-food store.
plain (all-purpose) unbleached wheat flour, is the best for baking: the gluten content ensures a strong dough, for a light result.
rice very fine, almost powdery, gluten-free flour; made from ground white rice. Used in baking, as a thickener, and in some Asian noodles and desserts. Another variety, made from glutinous sweet rice, is used for chinese dumplings and rice paper.
self-raising all-purpose plain or wholemeal flour with baking powder and salt added; make at home in the proportion of 1 cup plain or wholemeal flour to 2 teaspoons baking powder.
wholemeal also known as wholewheat flour; milled with the wheat germ so is higher in fibre and more nutritional than plain flour.

FOOD COLOURING vegetable-based substance available in liquid, paste or gel form.

FRUIT MINCE also known as mincemeat; mixture of dried fruits such as raisins, sultanas and candied peel, nuts, spices, apple, brandy or rum. Fruit mince is used as a filling for cakes, puddings and fruit mince pies.

GELATINE a thickening agent; we use dried (powdered) gelatine; it's also available in sheets known as leaf gelatine. Three teaspoons of dried gelatine (8g or one sachet) is about the same as four leaves.

GHEE (CLARIFIED BUTTER) with the milk solids removed, this fat has a high smoking point so can be heated to a high temperature without burning. Used as a cooking medium in most Indian recipes.

GINGER
fresh also called green or root ginger; the thick gnarled root of a tropical plant.
glacé fresh ginger root preserved in sugar syrup; crystallised ginger (sweetened with cane sugar) can be substituted if rinsed with warm water and dried before using.
ground also called powdered ginger; used as a flavouring in baking but cannot be substituted for fresh ginger.

GLACÉ FRUIT fruit such as pineapple, apricots, peaches and pears that are cooked in a heavy sugar syrup then dried.

GLUCOSE SYRUP also known as liquid glucose, made from wheat starch; used in jam and confectionery making. Available at health-food stores and supermarkets.

GOLDEN SYRUP a by-product of refined sugarcane; pure maple syrup or honey can be substituted. Treacle is more viscous, and has a stronger flavour and aroma than golden syrup.

GREASING/OILING PANS use butter or margarine (for sweet baking), oil or cooking-oil spray (for savoury baking) to grease baking pans; overgreasing pans can cause food to overbrown. Use absorbent paper or a pastry brush to spread the oil or butter over the pan. Try covering your hand with a small plastic bag then swiping it into the butter or margarine.

HAZELNUTS also known as filberts; plump, grape-sized, rich, sweet nut having a brown skin that is removed by rubbing heated nuts together vigorously in a tea-towel.
ground is made by grinding the hazelnuts to a coarse flour texture for use in baking or as a thickening agent.

HONEY the variety sold in a squeezable container is not suitable for the recipes in this book.

JAM also known as preserve or conserve; a thickened mixture of a fruit (and occasionally, a vegetable) and sugar.

LINSEEDS the seed from the flax plant. Mostly used to produce linseed oil, the grain is also used in bread.

LIQUEUR
blackcurrant-flavoured such as crème de cassis.
chocolate-flavoured such as crème de cacao.
coffee-flavoured such as kahlua or tia maria.
hazelnut-flavoured such as frangelico.
kirsch cherry-flavoured liqueur.
orange-flavoured such as curaçao, Grand Marnier or Cointreau.

MACADAMIAS native to Australia; fairly large, slightly soft, buttery rich nut. Should always be stored in the fridge to prevent their high oil content turning them rancid.

MAPLE-FLAVOURED SYRUP is made from sugar cane and is also called golden or pancake syrup. It is not a substitute for pure maple syrup.

MAPLE SYRUP also called pure maple syrup; distilled from the sap of sugar maple trees found only in Canada and the USA. Maple-flavoured syrup or pancake syrup is not an adequate substitute for the real thing.

MARMALADE a preserve, usually based on citrus fruit and its rind, cooked with sugar until the mixture has an intense flavour and thick consistency. Orange, lemon and lime are some of the commercially prepared varieties available.

MARSALA a fortified Italian wine produced in the region surrounding the Sicilian city of Marsala; recognisable by its intense amber colour and complex aroma. Often used in cooking, especially in sauces, risottos and desserts.

MARZIPAN made from ground almonds, sugar and glucose. Similar to almond paste but is not as strong in flavour; is finer in consistency and more pliable. Cheaper brands often use ground apricot kernels and sugar.

MILK
caramel top 'n' fill a canned milk product consisting of condensed milk that has been boiled to a caramel.
sweetened condensed a canned milk product consisting of milk with more than half the water content removed and sugar added to the remaining milk.

MIXED PEEL candied citrus peel.

MIXED SPICE a classic spice mixture generally containing caraway, allspice, coriander, cumin, nutmeg and ginger, although cinnamon and other spices can be added. It is used with fruit and in cakes.

MOLASSES a thick, dark brown syrup, the residue from the refining of sugar; available in light, dark and blackstrap varieties. Its slightly bitter taste is an essential ingredient in American cooking, found in foods such as gingerbread, shoofly pie and boston baked beans.

MUSCAT also known as muscatel; refers to both the grape variety and the sweet dessert wine made from them. The grape is superb eaten fresh; when dried, its distinctively musty flavour goes well with cheese, chocolate, pork and game.

MUSLIN inexpensive, undyed, finely woven cotton fabric called for in cooking to strain stocks and sauces; if unavailable, use disposable coffee filter papers.

NUTMEG a strong and pungent spice ground from the dried nut of an evergreen tree native to Indonesia. Usually found ground but the flavour is more intense from a whole nut, available from spice shops, so it's best to grate your own.

OIL
cooking spray we use a cholesterol-free cooking spray made from canola oil.
olive made from ripened olives. Extra virgin and virgin are the first and second press, respectively, of the olives and are therefore considered the best; "light" refers to taste not fat levels.
vegetable oils sourced from plant rather than animal fats.

ONIONS, BROWN AND WHITE are interchangeable, however white onions have a more pungent flesh.

ORANGE FLOWER WATER concentrated flavouring made from orange blossoms.

PASTRY
fillo paper-thin sheets of raw pastry; brush each sheet with oil or melted butter, stack in layers, then cut and fold as directed.
sheets ready-rolled packaged sheets of frozen puff and shortcrust pastry, available from supermarkets.

PEANUTS also known as groundnut, not in fact a nut but the pod of a legume. We mainly use raw (unroasted) or unsalted roasted peanuts.

PEPITAS the pale green kernels of dried pumpkin seeds; they can be bought plain or salted.

PINE NUTS also called pignoli; not a nut but a small, cream-coloured kernel from pine cones. They are best roasted before use to bring out the flavour.

PISTACHIOS green, delicately flavoured nuts inside hard off-white shells. Available salted or unsalted in their shells; you can also get them shelled.

POACHING a cooking term to describe gentle simmering of food in liquid (generally water or stock); spices or herbs can be added to impart their flavour.

POLENTA also known as cornmeal; a flour-like cereal made of dried corn (maize).

POPPY SEEDS small, dried, bluish-grey seeds of the poppy plant, with a crunchy texture and a nutty flavour. Can be purchased whole or ground in delicatessens and most supermarkets.

RAISINS dried sweet grapes (traditionally muscatel grapes).

RHUBARB a plant with long, green-red stalks; becomes sweet and edible when cooked.

ROASTING nuts and dried coconut can be roasted in the oven to restore their fresh flavour and release their aromatic essential oils. Spread them evenly onto an oven tray then roast in a moderate oven for about 5 minutes. Desiccated coconut, pine nuts and sesame seeds roast more evenly if stirred over low heat in a heavy-based frying pan; their natural oils will help turn them golden brown.

ROLLED OATS flattened oat grain rolled into flakes and traditionally used for porridge. Instant oats are also available, but use traditional oats for baking.

ROSEWATER extract made from crushed rose petals, called gulab in India; used for its aromatic quality in many sweetmeats and desserts.

SEGMENTING a cooking term to describe cutting citrus fruits in such a way that pieces contain no pith, seed or membrane. The peeled fruit is cut towards the centre inside each membrane, forming wedges.

SEMOLINA coarsely ground flour milled from durum wheat; the flour used in making gnocchi, pasta and couscous.

SESAME SEEDS black and white are the most common of this small oval seed, however there are also red and brown varieties. The seeds are used in cuisines the world over as an ingredient and as a condiment. Roast the seeds in a heavy-based frying pan over low heat.

SHERRY fortified wine consumed as an aperitif or used in cooking. Sherries differ in colour and flavour; sold as fino (light, dry), amontillado (medium sweet, dark) and oloroso (full-bodied, very dark).

SILVER BEET (SWISS CHARD) also called, incorrectly, spinach; has fleshy stalks and large leaves and can be prepared as for spinach.

SPINACH also called english spinach and incorrectly, silver beet. Baby spinach leaves are best eaten raw in salads; the larger leaves should be added last to soups, stews and stir-fries, and should be cooked until barely wilted.

STAR ANISE dried star-shaped pod with an astringent aniseed flavour; used to flavour stocks and marinades. Available whole and ground.

SUGAR
caster (superfine) finely granulated table sugar.
dark brown a moist, dark brown sugar with a rich, distinctive full flavour from molasses syrup.
demerara small-grained golden-coloured crystal sugar.
icing (confectioners') also known as powdered sugar; pulverised granulated sugar crushed together with a small amount of cornflour (cornstarch).
light brown a very soft, finely granulated sugar that retains molasses for its colour and flavour.
pure icing (confectioners') also known as powdered sugar.

raw natural brown granulated sugar.
vanilla is available in supermarkets, usually among the spices. Or, you can make your own by putting a couple of vanilla beans in a jar of caster sugar.
white (granulated) coarse, granulated table sugar, also known as crystal sugar.

SULTANAS also called golden raisins; dried seedless white grapes.

SUMAC a purple-red, astringent spice ground from berries growing on shrubs that flourish wild around the Mediterranean; adds a tart, lemony flavour to dips and dressings and goes well with barbecued meat. Can be found in Middle Eastern food stores.

SUNFLOWER SEEDS grey-green, slightly soft, oily kernels from sunflowers; a delicious and nutritious snack.

TREACLE thick, dark syrup not unlike molasses; a by-product of sugar refining.

TURMERIC also called kamin; is a rhizome related to galangal and ginger. Must be grated or pounded to release its acrid aroma and pungent flavour. Known for the golden colour it imparts, fresh turmeric can be substituted with the more commonly found dried powder. When fresh turmeric is called for, the dried powder can be substituted in the proportion of 1 teaspoon ground for every 20g (¾ ounce) fresh turmeric. Be aware that fresh turmeric stains your hands and plastic utensils such as chopping boards and spatulas.

VANILLA
bean dried, long, thin pod from a tropical golden orchid; the minuscule black seeds inside the bean impart a luscious flavour in baking and desserts. Place a whole bean in a jar of sugar to make vanilla sugar; a bean can be used three or four times.
paste made from vanilla beans and contains real seeds. Is highly concentrated – 1 teaspoon replaces a whole vanilla bean. Found in most supermarkets in the baking section.

VINEGAR
balsamic originally from Modena, Italy. Made from the juice of Trebbiano grapes; it is a deep rich brown colour with a sweet and sour flavour.
cider made from fermented apples.
malt made from fermented malt and beech shavings.
rice a colourless vinegar made from fermented rice and flavoured with sugar and salt. Sherry can be substituted.
white made from distilled grain alcohol.

YEAST (dried and fresh), a raising agent used in dough making. Granular (7g sachets) and fresh compressed (20g blocks) yeast can almost always be substituted for the other when yeast is called for.

YOGURT we use plain full-cream yogurt in our recipes.
Greek-style plain yogurt strained in a cloth (traditionally muslin) to remove the whey and to give it a creamy consistency.

ZUCCHINI also called courgette; small, pale- or dark-green or yellow vegetable of the squash family. Its edible flowers can be stuffed.

CONVERSION CHART

MEASURES

One Australian metric measuring cup holds approximately 250ml; one Australian metric tablespoon holds 20ml; one Australian metric teaspoon holds 5ml.

The difference between one country's measuring cups and another's is within a two- or three-teaspoon variance, and will not affect your cooking results. North America, New Zealand and the United Kingdom use a 15ml tablespoon.

All cup and spoon measurements are level. The most accurate way of measuring dry ingredients is to weigh them. When measuring liquids, use a clear glass or plastic jug with the metric markings.

The imperial measurements used in these recipes are approximate only. Measurements for cake pans are approximate only. Using same-shaped cake pans of a similar size should not affect the outcome of your baking. We measure the inside top of the cake pan to determine sizes.

We use large eggs with an average weight of 60g.

DRY MEASURES

METRIC	IMPERIAL
15g	½oz
30g	1oz
60g	2oz
90g	3oz
125g	4oz (¼lb)
155g	5oz
185g	6oz
220g	7oz
250g	8oz (½lb)
280g	9oz
315g	10oz
345g	11oz
375g	12oz (¾lb)
410g	13oz
440g	14oz
470g	15oz
500g	16oz (1lb)
750g	24oz (1½lb)
1kg	32oz (2lb)

LIQUID MEASURES

METRIC	IMPERIAL
30ml	1 fluid oz
60ml	2 fluid oz
100ml	3 fluid oz
125ml	4 fluid oz
150ml	5 fluid oz
190ml	6 fluid oz
250ml	8 fluid oz
300ml	10 fluid oz
500ml	16 fluid oz
600ml	20 fluid oz
1000ml (1 litre)	1¾ pints

LENGTH MEASURES

METRIC	IMPERIAL
3mm	⅛in
6mm	¼in
1cm	½in
2cm	¾in
2.5cm	1in
5cm	2in
6cm	2½in
8cm	3in
10cm	4in
13cm	5in
15cm	6in
18cm	7in
20cm	8in
22cm	9in
25cm	10in
28cm	11in
30cm	12in (1ft)

OVEN TEMPERATURES

The oven temperatures in this book are for conventional ovens; if you have a fan-forced oven, decrease the temperature by 10-20 degrees.

	°C (CELSIUS)	°F (FAHRENHEIT)
Very slow	120	250
Slow	150	300
Moderately slow	160	325
Moderate	180	350
Moderately hot	200	400
Hot	220	425
Very hot	240	475

INDEX

First published in 2013 by Bauer Media Books, Sydney
This edition first published in 2014.
Bauer Media Books are published by Bauer Media Limited.

BAUER
MEDIA GROUP

BAUER MEDIA BOOKS
Publisher Sally Wright
Editorial & food director Pamela Clark
Director of sales, marketing & rights Brian Cearnes
Creative director & designer Hieu Chi Nguyen
Senior editor Stephanie Kistner
Food concept director Sophia Young
Food editor Rebecca Meli
Marketing manager Bridget Cody
Senior business analyst Rebecca Varela
Business analyst Ashley Metcalfe
Operations manager David Scotto
Production controller Corinne Whitsun-Jones

Published by Bauer Media Books, a division of Bauer Media Ltd,
54 Park St, Sydney; GPO Box 4088, Sydney, NSW 2001.
phone (02) 9282 8618; fax (02) 9126 3702
www.awwcookbooks.com.au

Printed by 1010 Printing International Limited, China.

Australia Distributed by Network Services,
phone +61 2 9282 8777; fax +61 2 9264 3278;
networkweb@networkservicescompany.com.au
New Zealand Distributed by Bookreps NZ Ltd
phone +64 9 419 2635; fax +64 9 419 2634;
www.bookreps.co.nz
South Africa Distributed by PSD Promotions,
phone +27 11 392 6065/6/7; fax +27 11 392 6079/80;
orders@psdprom.co.za

A catalogue record for this book is available
from the National Library of Australia.
ISBN: 978-1-74245-524-2
© Bauer Media Ltd 2013
ABN 18 053 273 546

Cover photographer Louise Lister
Cover food stylist Yael Grinham
Cover photochef Sharon Kennedy

Photographer Louise Lister
Food stylist Jane Hann
Photochef Kerrie Ray

To order books phone 136 116 (within Australia) or
order online at www.awwcookbooks.com.au
Send recipe enquiries to:
recipeenquiries@bauer-media.com.au